CHALLENGES & OPPORTUNITIES

FOR BUSINESS IN
POST-APARTHEID SOUTH AFRICA

INVESTOR RESPONSIBILITY RESEARCH CENTER, INC.

CHALLENGES & OPPORTUNITIES

FOR BUSINESS IN
POST-APARTHEID SOUTH AFRICA

EDITED BY

MEG VOORHES

INVESTOR RESPONSIBILITY RESEARCH CENTER, INC.

The Investor Responsibility Research Center compiles and impartially analyzes information on the activities of business in society, on activities of institutional investors, on efforts to influence such activities, and on related public policies. IRRC's publications and other services are available by subscription or individually. IRRC's work is financed primarily by annual subscription fees paid by more than 400 investing institutions for the Social Issues Service, the Corporate Governance Service, the South Africa Review Service, the Environmental Information Service and the Global Shareholder Service. This edited transcript is a publication of the South Africa Review Service. The Center was founded in 1972 as an independent, not-for-profit corporation. It is governed by a 21-member board of directors who represent subscribing institutions.

Executive Director: Margaret Carroll
Director, South Africa Review Service: Meg Voorhes

ISBN 1-879775-18-2

TABLE OF CONTENTS

PREFACE

On October 12, 1993, the Investor Responsibility Research Center held a conference in Washington, D.C., that drew together approximately 100 representatives from corporations, institutional investors, U.S. government agencies and other organizations to discuss the *Challenges and Opportunities for Business in Post-Apartheid South Africa.* The conference came in the wake of several political breakthroughs in South Africa in its transition to democracy, and shortly before U.S. Commerce Secretary Ronald Brown led a trade mission to South Africa and before several major U.S. companies, including some that were represented at the conference, announced new business ventures in South Africa.

What follows is an edited transcript of the formal presentations of the 15 speakers. Material in brackets has been added by the editor for the purposes of clarification and updating.

This transcript was edited by Meg Voorhes, the director of IRRC's South Africa Review Service, and prepared for publication by Phyllis W. Johnson. Beth Singer Design designed the cover.

WELCOMING REMARKS

MEG VOORHES

Good morning. Welcome to IRRC's conference on the *Challenges and Opportunities for Business in Post-Apartheid South Africa*. As the director of IRRC's South Africa Review Service, I am delighted to have you all here today.

We are meeting at a particularly appropriate time to discuss the post-apartheid era. In the last two weeks, South Africa's Parliament has passed legislation to create a transitional executive council, Nelson Mandela has called for the lifting of economic sanctions against South Africa, and the United Nations has urged the nations of the world to heed his call.

Several years before these dramatic events, at a time when Mandela seemed destined to die in prison, I saw Athol Fugard's play, *A Lesson from Aloes*, performed here in Washington. The central character uttered a statement that electrified me then and has stayed with me ever since: "An evil system isn't a natural disaster. There's nothing you can do to stop a drought, but bad laws and social injustice are manmade and can be unmade by men."

We are now witnessing the unmaking of apartheid. It has been unmade by internal and external pressures, by mass movements and the actions of individuals. The legal edifice—the influx control and segregation laws—has fallen away. The political structure is rapidly falling away, although the emerging post-apartheid political order is fragile and threatened by violence. The unmaking of economic apartheid, however, promises to be a challenge even greater than forging the post-apartheid political order has proven to be so far, and this challenge will occupy much of our discussion today.

Of course, the political and economic spheres cannot be discussed separately; they are interlinked. Many observers worry, legitimately, how a post-apartheid government can improve the material position of the millions of black South Africans who are undereducated and un- or underemployed. Clearly, any political order will be fragile in a country where 45 percent of the population is unemployed by the formal company, as is the case in South Africa today.

Our speakers this morning will explore these political and economic challenges—particularly the central challenge of black economic empowerment—in greater detail from their knowledgeable and independent perspectives. The speakers on our afternoon panels will focus more on the opportunities mentioned in the title of this conference. Specifically, they will discuss projects and

---

Meg Voorhes is the director of the South Africa Review Service at IRRC.

initiatives in which they have taken part that are helping to improve the economic status of black South Africans; they will present ideas that U.S. and other multinational companies can participate in or emulate in their South African operations.

However, for many U.S. companies that are considering whether to expand their business ties to South Africa, a critical question is the status of policy at home towards companies doing business in South Africa. We have asked U.S. Secretary of Commerce Ron Brown to discuss the policy directions of the current administration in this regard. And IRRC senior analyst Bill Moses, the author of our annual guides to American state and local laws on South Africa, will discuss the current status of these state and local sanctions and the prospects for their repeal.

Thus, I believe we have an excellent and very informative program set up for you today. We have scheduled time throughout the day to allow for the speakers to take your questions from the floor, so I hope you will not be shy about taking advantage of this opportunity.

Finally, before I introduce our keynote speaker, I would like to say a few words about IRRC, for those of you who may be unfamiliar with the Investor Responsibility Research Center. IRRC was founded in 1972 by a group of U.S. institutional investors to conduct impartial research on public policy issues that have an impact on corporations and institutional shareholders. Today, more than 500 institutional investors, corporations, law firms, government agencies and other organizations subscribe to IRRC's five subscription services, including the South Africa Review Service, which was launched in 1978.

The South Africa Review Service provides indepth analysis of the evolving political situation and investment climate in South Africa. Given the dramatic recent developments in South Africa, we plan to expand our coverage of portfolio social investing in South Africa and of affirmative action and development issues relevant to multinational companies doing business there.

Once again, I and my colleagues at IRRC extend you a warm welcome; we appreciate your interest in the *Challenges and Opportunites for Business in Post-Apartheid South Africa.*

BEYOND THE ELECTION
THE CHALLENGES FACING SOUTH AFRICA

MAMPHELA RAMPHELE

I want to thank IRRC for providing us, as South Africans, with this opportunity to come and share with you some of the anguishes, the hopes, and the dreams that we've got for our country. My task this morning is to talk very openly about the challenges that are facing us in the pre- and post-election period in South Africa.

The South African transitional process has humbled many analysts. Various scenarios have been sketched over the last few years in an attempt to look into the future in a more systematic way. But even scenario expertise has been severely tested by the multiplicity of factors one has to take into account to arrive at some reasonable understanding of the prospects lying in store for change in South Africa.

Major factors affecting South Africa

Thus, I will do no more today than to give you my own sense of what kind of future scenarios the current transitional process is likely to deliver to South Africa. In my assessment, I've taken several factors into consideration.

The legacy of the past: First, the legacy of the past, with its inequity, racism, sexism and blatant trampling on the human dignity of the majority of South Africans, is bound to have serious implications for the future. The bitter fruits of this legacy cannot be wished away: broken families; high illiteracy rates—variously estimated between 50 and 56 percent; and high unemployment rates—varying from 30 to 60 percent, depending on what part of the country one is looking at.

According to a study by the Community Agency for Social Enquiry, which was commissioned by the Joint Enrichment Project of the South African Council of Churches and the South African Catholic Bishops' Conference, many youths in South Africa are frustrated. Fifty-six percent of them are unemployed. Only 12 percent of African youths have studied as far as they wanted to go, and 59 percent of all youths feel that they cannot realize their full potential.

That's a very serious state of affairs for a nation intending to change.

In addition, there is a general lack of trust between people in South Africa and a fear of the unknown.

Mamphela Ramphele is the deputy vice chancellor of the University of Cape Town, where she is responsible for the implementation of the university's equity policies.

South Africans also lack the experience of good governance and public accountability that is essential to keeping those in positions of authority in check. Because South Africa has never in its entire history had a democratic government, it is going to entail very serious learning by all of us if we're going to get it right.

Revolutionary rhetoric: The second factor that I've taken into consideration in addition to this legacy is that a significant sector of the youth, particularly among Africans, feel that they were robbed of a victorious revolution. The storming of the Bastille was (in their view) in sight, if only the besuited gentlemen had not decided to settle around a table and negotiate. They feel that the negotiators have betrayed this revolution.

The reality, of course, is very different. There was no real prospect of a dramatic, victorious revolution, but the liberation movement, as was its historical responsibility, kept the mythology of the revolution alive until very recently. Indeed, the Pan-Africanist Congress and Azapo still feed false expectations with their rhetoric. Yet talk about transfer of power as the only basis for negotiations were common until only about a year ago. It is thus understandable that young people would continue to hanker after a revolution that never could be.

Desire for peace and prosperity: The third factor I've taken into consideration is that in spite of the above, the majority of black South Africans and white South Africans, young and old, urban and rural, of whatever political party, desire nothing more than a peaceful transition to a democratic and prosperous future. The definition of "prosperous" is in the minds of the majority of these people a realistic one. Even for those on the edge of survival, few would expect more than being given the opportunity to succeed in the medium and long term. Thus, the expectations of the majority of people in South Africa are realistic and reasonable.

Unrealistic expectations, however, are in evidence among the elite in the black community, both young and old, and also among white people who have unrealistic expectations about maintaining a life of privilege. Some of the calls for redress have not necessarily been focused on the majority. It is unfortunately true that the benefits of transition will flow along the existing contours of privilege.

Support for negotiations: The fourth factor I've taken into consideration is that the great majority of people in South Africa support the existing negotiation process. The majority of the participants have come to realize that if they do not put their minds to finding reasonable compromises, there would be no country to fight over.

The tendency to stage walkouts whenever the going got tough or when some national tragedy occurred has given way to greater determination to forge ahead in spite of, or even because of setbacks. Only those on the extreme right, both black and white, still believe they can afford the luxury of throwing out their toys whenever they do not get their way.

I thus believe that the period leading up to the elections will reflect the tensions generated by the relative strengths of these four factors and of other factors which drive the transitional process in South Africa. But central to successful transition would have to be visionary leadership with a capacity to hold the middle ground together.

It should also be borne in mind that unlike many societies undergoing transition, South Africans have creatively dealt with the question of creating legitimate and credible institutions to guide the process and to mediate between the parties in conflict. The contribution of the Goldstone Commission, the National Peace Committee, the Peace Accord, and more recently the Independent Electoral Commission and the Joint Peacekeeping Force and Independent Media Commissions all hold promise in diffusing tensions in the months ahead.

The likely scenarios

So with these factors in mind, I will now go on to look at what are the likely scenarios in the pre- and post-election period.

Like Burke, I will suspend my congratulations on the liberation of South Africa until I am informed about "how well it had been combined with good government, with public order, with the discipline and obedience of armies, with the collection of an effective and well distributed revenue, with morality and religion, with the solidity of property, with peace and order, with civil manners."

I would like to paint three scenarios as a method of looking at prospects in the pre- and post-election period. Each one reflects a different balance of the factors outlined above. The first scenario is a successful transition with prosperity, and I'll call that the "Prosperity Scenario." The second one is successful transition to democracy but little prosperity. I'll call that the "Stagnation Scenario." The third one is transition to democracy with chaos, and I'll call that the "Chaos Scenario."

The Prosperity Scenario: Let's start with the good news and look at the Prosperity Scenario. The elements of this Scenario are drawn from objective observation of current trends in our society which center around the following four elements.

First, the continued negotiation between the major political players and their determination to iron out differences through various deadlock breaking mechanisms, such as bilateral meetings, technical committees and use of honest brokers.

Successes have been achieved as evidenced by the agreements on the election date, the Transitional Executive Council, the Independent Electoral Commission, Independent Media Commission, et cetera. Outstanding issues such as the interim Constitution, the Bill of Rights, regional boundaries, look set to be resolved in time for the November session of Parliament.

The second element of the Scenario is the equally important negotiations occurring around socioeconomic issues and involving the major stakeholders—the government, the private sector, labor and non-governmental organizations. These negotiations occur in fora established to tackle specific problem areas. We've got an Economic Forum, a Housing Forum, a Health Forum, education and training fora, youth development fora, drought relief fora — you name it.

I don't think there is another country in this world undergoing transformation which has gone this route, and I believe that the social compacts informed by the emergence of a shared vision of the future are the desired outcomes of these efforts, and they're likely to make an enormous contribution to stabilizing the process of transformation.

The third element is the development efforts by many South Africans which have kept hope alive amongst the very poor. But independent development has also enabled the poor to conceive of themselves as active agents of history. This empowerment process can only have a positive impact on the quality of social relations in the future and on the capacity of ordinary people to govern.

The ANC Freedom Charter says the people shall govern, and I think it's a very important cry to rally people together. But it's important that people learn to govern, and the independent development process that's going on at different levels in South Africa is an important ingredient in this learning to govern. It is, after all, ordinary South Africans who must put the limits on those in positions of authority by demanding public accountability at all levels. The extent to which the independence of development is protected from the vicissitudes of party political interests will determine the level of success in tackling the major challenges facing us.

The fourth element is that in spite of, or perhaps because of, the level of blood-letting in our streets, in the farms and in the villages of South Africa, there is a growing peace movement in our land. People from all walks of life are linking hands to say no to violence. It is gratifying to see the triumph of the human spirit above the hatred and divisions nurtured by past governments of South Africa to protect white minority rule. Thus, a shared vision of the future is also being forged amongst ordinary people in this peace movement.

An important aspect of ordinary people's lives is their work environment. Employment equity has to be a major focus of the transitional process, and it is gratifying to see how many firms, private and public, in South Africa are taking employment equity very seriously. By employment equity I refer to three major aspects:

- First, increasing access to employment opportunities for blacks and women;
- Second, ensuring optimal personal development for those who participate in the economic process;
- And third, changing the institutional culture that characterizes public and private organizations in South Africa.

With respect to increasing access to employment opportunities, it's very easy to say, "There are no qualified blacks and women; therefore, we will continue to employ white males." The fact of the matter is, if one really has creative recruitment and selection procedures, you can identify people with potential and bring them in for the second level, which is ensuring optimum personal development for those who are brought into the institutions.

I believe that that personal development includes the willingness of public and private firms to invest money in education and training for those who have been disadvantaged by past practices and legislation. For example, we don't have many black engineers in South Africa, but by systematic investment in the training of black engineers, there has been a significant increase in the number of successful graduates from both the University of Witwatersrand and the University of Cape Town, as well as Natal. So I don't believe that it is impossible to change the current profile of top management structures in South Africa.

Third, a very important part of the process of employment equity is changing the institutional culture that governs public and private organizations, because the institutional culture, if it is to nurture personal development, has to reflect greater diversity and to increase the quality of life for all those who are employed within that institution.

I believe that a good equal opportunity employer is good for all, including white males, because it leads to an increase in the quality of their lives. A change in paradigm towards a people-centered development process will allow for drawing in the energy of blacks and women to relieve the overburdened white male leadership of the impossible task of carrying a disproportionate responsibility for the development of the whole of humanity.

An employment equity policy framework is thus very different from an affirmative action one. I believe that affirmative action is a strategy for achieving employment equity. I get concerned when people see affirmative action as the policy, the program, because it begs the question as to who is affirming whom for what purpose. So we need to define an employment equity policy framework within which affirmative action would be a useful and a well-designed strategy.

I believe we should learn from Canada and to some extent from Australia where the focus is on employment equity. In your country you have opted more for an affirmative action approach, and I think you have had mixed results. One cannot expect much success if new entrants have not got the space to redefine the culture of the institutions they're entering. Resentment is the likely outcome from both sides.

South Africans have an opportunity to define the whole policy environment into which the country is moving. The success with which it does go appropriately will determine the extent to which it releases the creative energy of the majority of South Africans to participate in the national reconstruction process.

Provided that the above developments hold and are strengthened, one can reasonably anticipate a successful transition with assured prosperity to be marked by socioeconomic hardship in the short term for the majority of people, given the backlogs in the provision of basic needs in housing, education, health and employment. But in the medium and long term, I believe that it is possible for South Africa to begin to show very considerable strides towards a more prosperous socioeconomic environment.

So that's the good news about the Prosperity Scenario.

The Stagnation Scenario: I would be dishonest if I didn't explore with you the possibility of the Stagnation Scenario.

This remains a realistic scenario, given global and historical precedents. South Africans, like other social actors, may refuse to learn from history, but want to make their own mistakes. Two factors are likely to drive this Scenario: first, right-wing violence, and second, populist pressure.

The right, which in our country consists of both white and blacks, is prepared to, and has demonstrated its ability to, use violence to prevent a successful transition. The ambivalence of the government in dealing with right-wing violence and the alleged continued collaboration of some elements of the state security machinery with killer squads has created space for this threat to grow and for the leaders of these groups to grow in confidence.

For example, how does one explain the AWB [a right-wing white group] bravado of storming the World Trade Center [where the multiparty negotiations took place]? They are spoilers who have vested interests in the status quo. Unless the Transitional Executive Council takes a firm stand on this issue, these spoilers present the greatest threat to the future of South Africa.

Second, the utopian views of some liberation movements on the left of the ANC may put pressure on the future government to pursue populist policies. The lack of realism about what is feasible in the sphere of redressing the inequities of the past is understandable. The cruel irony of history is that those who benefited from the inequities of the past, including homeland leaders and

National Party officials who have been shown to have been corrupt in the extreme, are likely to continue to enjoy the spoils of their past occupations.

This is a bitter pill for a lot of political activists to swallow, but it has to be swallowed. Unless there is a greater willingness to make serious commitments to setting up mechanisms for redress for victims of forced removals, deaths in detention and other nefarious acts of the past, it is difficult to imagine a meaningful reconciliation occurring in South Africa. The call to let bygones be bygones can only make sense if there is full public disclosure of past wrongdoing. Otherwise, bitterness and anger will continue to fester like an infected wound until the underlying past is opened up and cleaned out.

In this Scenario, one can expect the pre- and post-election period to be marked by continuing violence, lack of investor confidence, and significant flight of capital and skills. A government of national unity may be able to contain the violence through extraordinary measures such as states of emergency, but the uneasy order established under such circumstances is unlikely to be sustainable unless the space that is created thereby is regarded as a window of opportunity to address the underlying socioeconomic problems.

The Chaos Scenario: As if that is not enough, there is still the Chaos Scenario. There are a number of factors which have the potential to connive to make this Scenario a reality.

First, the growing confidence of the right-wing and the escalating indiscriminate violence that it seems to unleash in strategic areas whenever major breakthroughs are made at the negotiation table are very disturbing. The unwillingness of the South African security forces to act with the same vigor and determination that they have displayed and continue to display when dealing with black protestors or blacks violating law and order provisions is a major factor in giving space for white right-wing violence.

Second, the continued unwillingness of homeland governments to relinquish control over areas of South Africa as part of the pre-election preparations poses a serious problem. Rural communities are being held hostage by cheap personalized politics which employ ethnic and other symbolic metaphors to justify their claims to power.

Third, the continued "armed struggle" of the Pan-Africanist Congress plays into the hands of, and fuels, white-right wing violence by giving it a pseudo-moral justification. Random attacks on whites are just as despicable as attacks on blacks. [In January 1994, the leadership of the Pan-Africanist Congress announced that the organization was suspending the armed struggle.]

Fourth, the continued social disintegration—and the deterioration of the moral base of social relationships—poses a danger to prospects for reconstruction. South Africans have little chance of being competitive internationally unless their human resource base is considerably strengthened. Little benefit can be derived from increased investment in education, housing, job creation, if not accompanied by a change in the mindset of all towards a greater commitment to excellence of performance at all levels.

The above factors in varying combinations are likely to lead to an increase in violent conflict, loss of business and other confidence, flight of skills and capital. A government of national unity would not have the capacity to halt this, once the decline starts gaining momentum.

Conclusion

In conclusion, I maintain that the Prosperity Scenario remains a real possibility in South Africa. There is a sufficient critical mass at the center which can be held together successfully through creative, visionary leadership. Socioeconomic development would have to be pursued with vigor to underpin the political transitional process. Increased investment by South Africans in the first instance would be a vote of confidence in the future of their own country. Investment by the international community, both private and public, both financially and in terms of skills, is essential to invigorating our ailing economy.

The Stagnation and Chaos Scenarios are not inevitable. The international community could play an important role in supporting successful transition in South Africa by helping to frustrate the possible linkage of the right-wing with international networks of support. Positive support in moral and material terms for the pre-election, election and post-election monitoring process would limit the chances of the credibility and legitimacy of the fairness of the elections being questioned.

South Africans are going through a crucial historical period which could usher in a prosperous future not only for the country but for the sub-Saharan region as a whole. But like any change process, there is both opportunity and danger encapsulated in a single historical moment. The outcome depends on seizing the opportunity and minimizing the danger.

I believe that South Africans have what it takes to make it.

SOUTH AFRICA'S ECONOMY
TO THE YEAR 2000

AZAR JAMMINE

Good morning to you, ladies and gentlemen. And thank you very much to IRRC for inviting me to address you. It is indeed an honor.

We've got to talk about the economy to the year 2000. Well, the economy from the year 1960 has not been one of all that much to write home about. As you can see, in general, we have been going downhill for over 30 years [Chart 1].

I'd like to separate my mini-presentation into two sections: one to talk about the medium-term, what we have had over the past four years of recession, and what we're likely to see over the next two to three years looking ahead. And then, looking further ahead, what do we need to do to change this very long-term downward trend.

The short-term view

Now, the positive thing you will notice is that from the very short-term point of view, things amazingly are actually getting worse very much more slowly than they were a little while ago, and there is reason to believe matters will continue improving [Table 1].

And that is, to a certain extent, quite surprising, bearing in mind all the violence and political uncertainty that is taking place. Let me just give you a couple of examples: the growth in retail sales. You can see, a year ago the economy was about to fall totally down the cliff, and yet, ever since negotiations resumed in September last year, the rate of decline has got smaller and smaller, despite Chris Hani's assassination [Chart 2].

Manufacturing production, the same kind of pattern you can see. We're still not growing, but at least we're not declining, despite all the upheaval on the political front that has been taking place [Chart 3].

And, a variable very close to American's hearts, car sales — look how they're growing, faster than at any stage over the past four years [Chart 4]. So, despite everything on the political front, the economy is actually doing its own thing. And, it is likely to continue picking up, because we have had a significant decline in interest rates over the past two to three years. For a good three years, our interest rates remained above 20 percent, but they're down to 15, 16 percent right now.

(continued on page 20)

Azar Jammine is the executive director and chief economist of Econometrix (Pty.) Ltd., South Africa's leading private, independent economic research and consulting company.

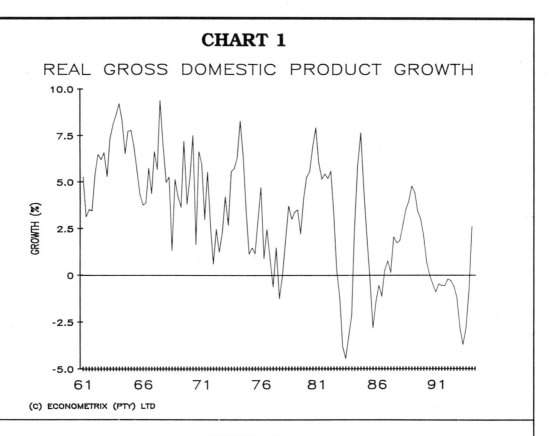

CHART 1

REAL GROSS DOMESTIC PRODUCT GROWTH

(C) ECONOMETRIX (PTY) LTD

TABLE 1
WHY 1995/96 COULD SEE A BOOM

- BUSINESS CYCLE LOOKS TO BE BOTTOMING
- IMPACT OF DROUGHT WILL HAVE DISSIPATED
- WORLD ECONOMY SHOULD BE RECOVERING
- GOLD PRICE IN BULL TREND
- WAGE INCREASES HIGHER THAN INFLATION
- IMPROVED BALANCE SHEETS FROM LOWER INTEREST RATES
- INVENTORY REPLENISHMENT
- IMF AND WORLD BANK LOANS
- FUNDS DIRECTED AT SOCIAL UPLIFTMENT
- MEGA CAPITAL PROJECTS

POSSIBLE CONSTRAINTS

- POLITICAL DEVELOPMENTS
- INCREASED TAXATION
- REDUCED GOVERNMENT CONSUMPTION

18

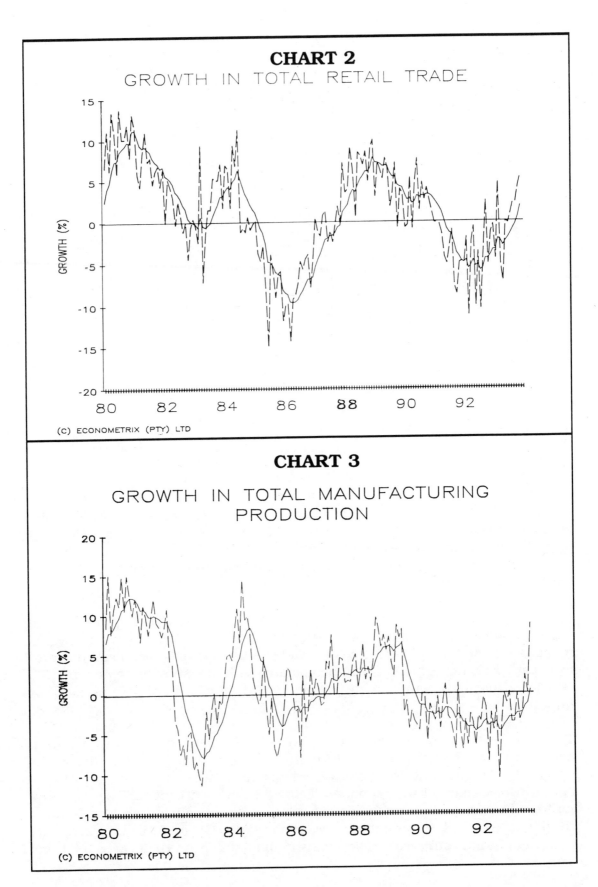

CHART 2
GROWTH IN TOTAL RETAIL TRADE

(C) ECONOMETRIX (PTY) LTD

CHART 3

GROWTH IN TOTAL MANUFACTURING PRODUCTION

(C) ECONOMETRIX (PTY) LTD

19

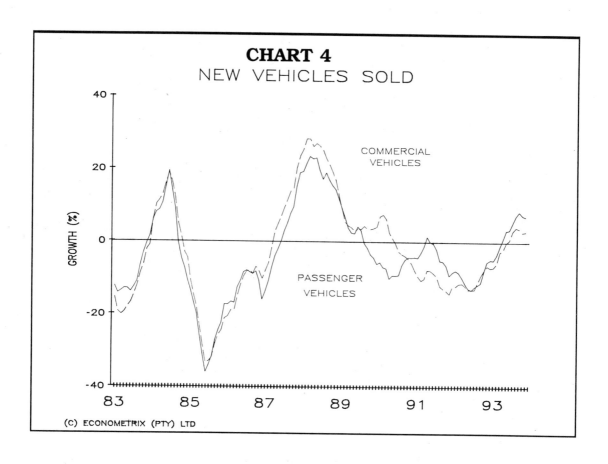

CHART 4

NEW VEHICLES SOLD

GROWTH (%)

COMMERCIAL VEHICLES

PASSENGER VEHICLES

(C) ECONOMETRIX (PTY) LTD

And, in many respects, we share some of the characteristics that are common to the United States. We also had a massive credit boom in the late 1980s. And we have had to have a tight monetary policy, high interest rates to break the back of that credit boom. And we have succeeded in doing so. In so doing, we have succeeded in bringing down the inflation rate from about 16 or 17 percent, to single digits [Chart 5].

So, you can see that the base is being formed for a reasonable improvement in the economy. The rate of insolvencies is starting to come down in lagged response to the fall in interest rates. And stock levels have been run down so low that there are signs now that people are gradually starting to pick up and reorder [Chart 6]. And so, the economy, despite everything, is actually improving.

There are welcome indications that a number of other factors that have been depressing the economy are beginning to change in our favor. One is the dreadful drought that we experienced in the summer rainfall regions — agriculture's share of the economy declined from 6 percent to 3 percent in a matter of a year. But, I can tell you that last week was absolutely wonderful. I think in the United States if it rains everyone says, "Ooooh." Well, I can assure you, in Johannesburg last week, everyone had smiles on their faces as it just

20

CHART 5
SOUTH AFRICAN INFLATION RATE

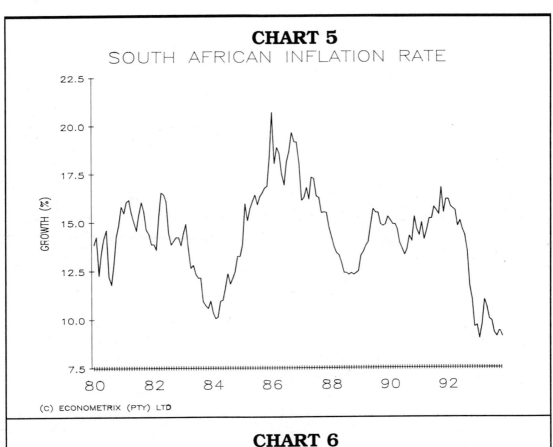

CHART 6
COMMERCIAL & INDUSTRIAL INVENTORIES
AS % OF GROSS DOMESTIC PRODUCT

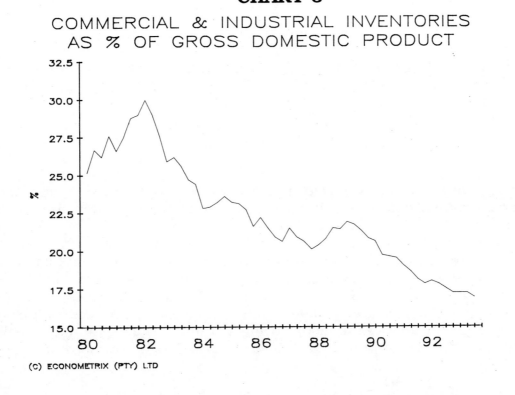

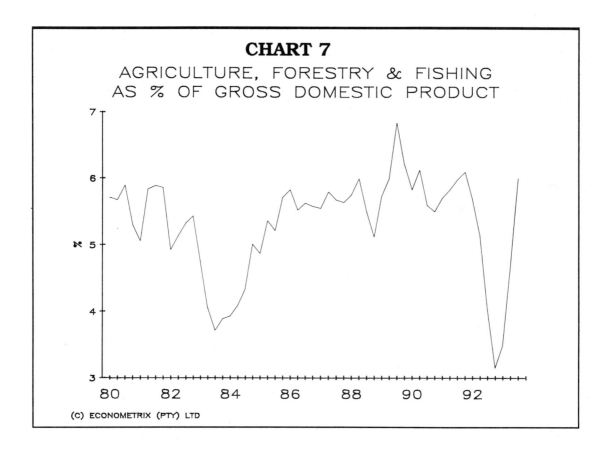

CHART 7

AGRICULTURE, FORESTRY & FISHING
AS % OF GROSS DOMESTIC PRODUCT

(C) ECONOMETRIX (PTY) LTD

kept pouring with rain. And this is starting to be reflected in terms of an improvement in the economy [Chart 7].

Unfortunately, we are also very dependent on yourselves to get the U.S. economy to pick up, you can see the very close relationship between South Africa's economy and the economies of its leading trading partners—the United States, the United Kingdom, Germany and Japan. Fortunately, there are signs that the average of the overall economies overseas are gradually picking up [Charts 8 and 9].

And then, finally, we have the gold price, especially in terms of a devaluing rand, has risen quite significantly in the past three to six months, and that also should see us through quite well [Charts 10 and 11].

So, the natural business cycle is picking up, and superimposed on that is the possibility that we will have a relatively peaceful political transition. Add to this that our foreign debt is as low as it's ever been [Charts 12 and 13] (and as a developing country we're very underborrowed) and you can see the confluence of factors that could lead to money being lent to the country and to a really significant upswing starting to take hold once the general elections are out of the way.

22

CHART 8

S.A. REAL GROSS DOMESTIC PRODUCT GROWTH VS G4 INDUSTRIAL PRODUCTION GROWTH

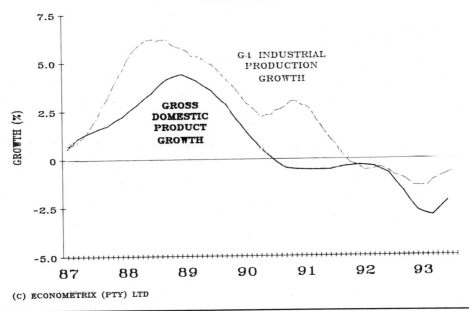

(C) ECONOMETRIX (PTY) LTD

CHART 9

G4 INDUSTRIAL PRODUCTION GROWTH VS COMMODITY PRICE INDEX : METALS

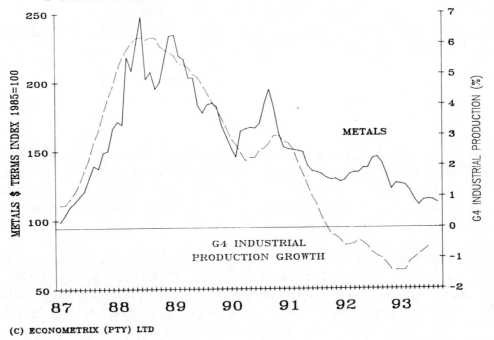

(C) ECONOMETRIX (PTY) LTD

23

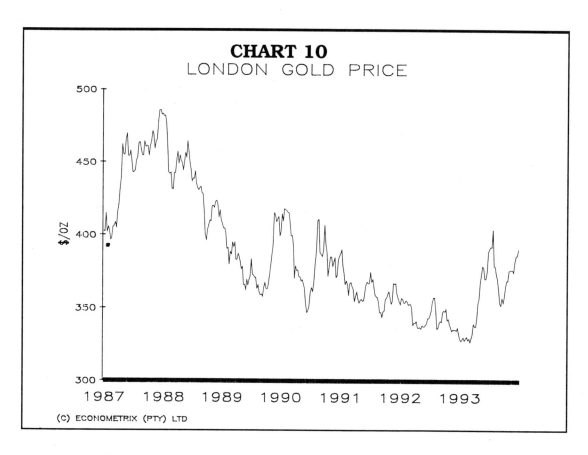

CHART 10
LONDON GOLD PRICE

(C) ECONOMETRIX (PTY) LTD

Sustaining the economic upturn

So I'm fairly positive that 1995-96 will see the most prosperous time for the South African economy that we will have seen since 1987-88. The question is: Will the economy be able to convert this window of opportunity provided by such an upswing into something more sustainable.

I would like to suggest that there are several areas of opportunity in South Africa that could make it the leading developing country of the world. They fall into three categories.

1) While apartheid has created a lot of ills and a lot of inequalities, the alleviation of those very inequalities will create opportunities for economic growth. By providing massive housing schemes, education, health and electrification, and by upgrading transport facilities, a multitude of industries are fit to benefit, and to benefit in an enormous way.

2) The second area of opportunity I believe is in the potential development of black entrepreneurship. Until the mid-1980s, blacks were prohibited by law from running businesses the way they would like to. Since then we have had a process of deregulation, and we have seen the growth of a burgeoning informal sector second to none, which is starting to manifest an innate desire to do business and to embark upon entrepreneurship amongst many blacks.

24

CHART 11
GOLD PRICE IN RAND TERMS

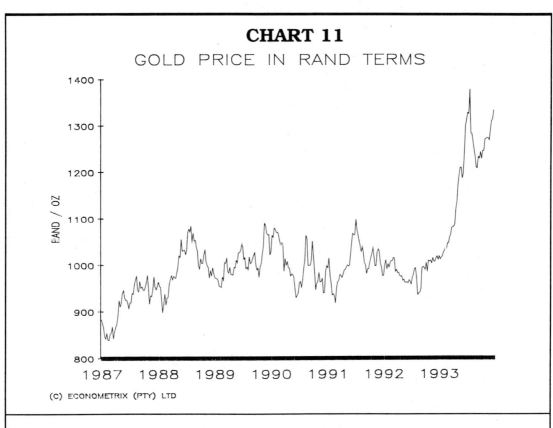

CHART 12
TOTAL FOREIGN DEBT AS % OF GROSS DOMESTIC PRODUCT

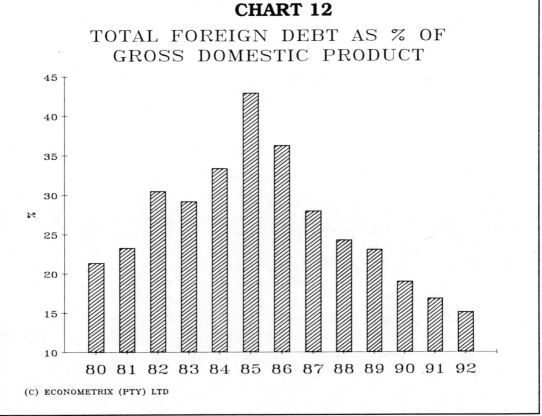

25

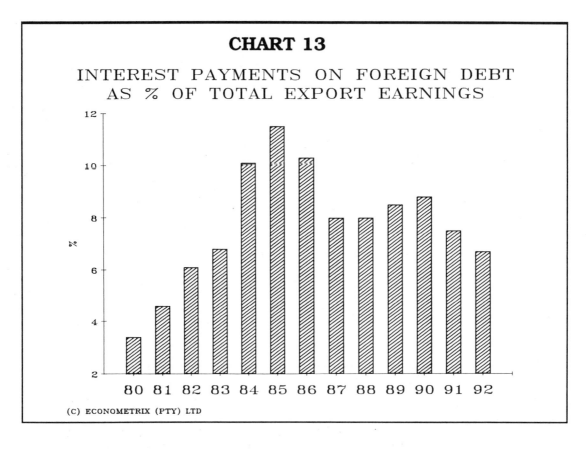

CHART 13

INTEREST PAYMENTS ON FOREIGN DEBT AS % OF TOTAL EXPORT EARNINGS

(C) ECONOMETRIX (PTY) LTD

The extent of that black entrepreneurship at this stage is minuscule. However, to get half a million or a million black entrepreneurs really and truly doing business, I think, would send the South African economy soaring ahead. There is a huge internal consumer market out there, 40 million people.

3) And, in addition, I believe that there is an enormous opportunity to use South Africa not only as a base for entering and trading with the rest of Africa, but also to help in the development and exploitation of the country's own infrastructure, which is extremely highly developed by international developing country standards.

We have a very good telecommunications network. It's easy to call the country. Road and transport networks are very sophisticated. And above all, we have a very sophisticated financial network, a financial sector equal to all those in the top Western countries.

So, there is the opportunity to use and develop the First World side of the economy, as well as the Third World side of the economy, in a kind of combination that I think is fairly unique in the world at the moment.

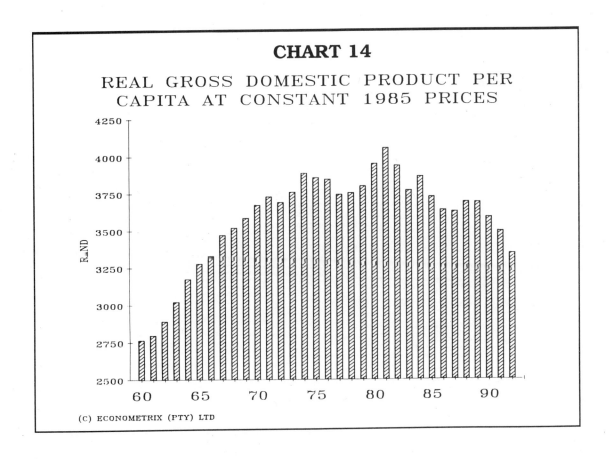

CHART 14

REAL GROSS DOMESTIC PRODUCT PER CAPITA AT CONSTANT 1985 PRICES

(C) ECONOMETRIX (PTY) LTD

Sanctions

Now, many people will say, "Well, surely, now the floodgates are open; economic sanctions have been lifted." However, I would like to remind you, first and foremost, that the economy began slowing down back around 1965, 1970 — long before sanctions became a major issue, which was in the mid-1980s [Chart 14].

So, in other words, there was a lot that was going wrong with the economy long before sanctions really became a major issue. And I would therefore suggest that while sanctions may have had a psychological impact, they were not the only factor by far to have forced this economy to turn around.

And even then, take trade sanctions. A lot of people have this perception that they did a lot of harm to the economy, yet, if you look at the volume of exports since sanctions were imposed, it's been growing quite nicely, thank you very much [Chart 15]. The country's been able to bypass many of those sanctions.

The other argument is that financial sanctions have done a tremendous amount of harm, because it is said the country has had to restrict growth in imports in order to generate enough foreign exchange with which to repay foreign debts. The argument is that South Africa was forced to run a surplus on the current

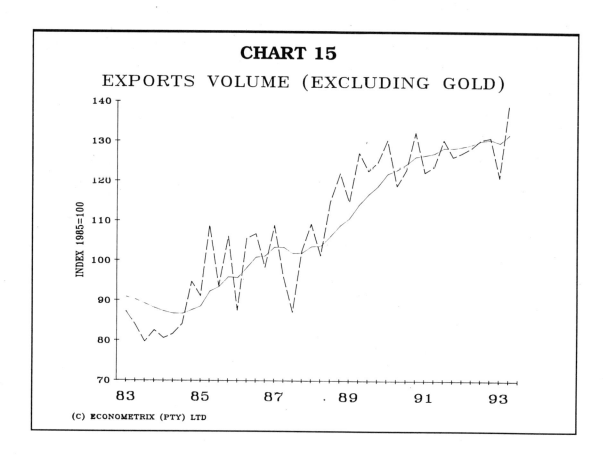

CHART 15

EXPORTS VOLUME (EXCLUDING GOLD)

INDEX 1985=100

(C) ECONOMETRIX (PTY) LTD

account of the balance of payments—to export more than it could import—in order to earn foreign exchange with which to meet its foreign debt repayments.

Again, this is hardly true. I believe that the main reason why we've been able to run the current account surplus [Chart 16] is because the economy has been weak for other structural reasons, which have made import levels grow so slowly in line with the close correlation between imports and the level of economic activity [Chart 17] that we've actually been able to generate enough foreign exchange, irrespective of the access to foreign capital from abroad.

It is really only in 1993, this particular year, that I believe sanctions have done more harm to the economy than at any other stage, because despite a relatively weak economy, the drought and the need to increase our foreign debt repayments this particular year has forced the level of gold and foreign exchanges reserves downwards very sharply. [Chart 18] This, in turn, has compelled the Central Bank to keep interests rates higher than they would otherwise have done in the middle of a recession.

And unfortunately, our debt repayments are going to be huge for the next five years as well, [Chart 19] running on the order of $2 billion per annum. And that is why, that is the principal reason why we need IMF funds at the moment, because otherwise we will have to keep our interest rates extremely high.

28

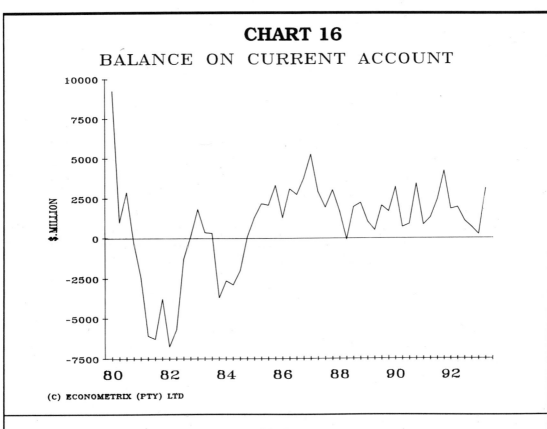

CHART 16
BALANCE ON CURRENT ACCOUNT

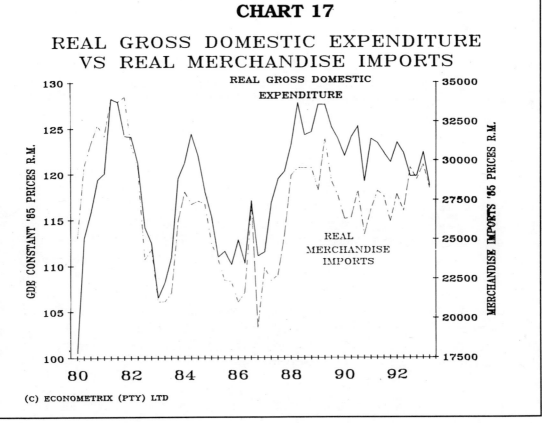

CHART 17

REAL GROSS DOMESTIC EXPENDITURE
VS REAL MERCHANDISE IMPORTS

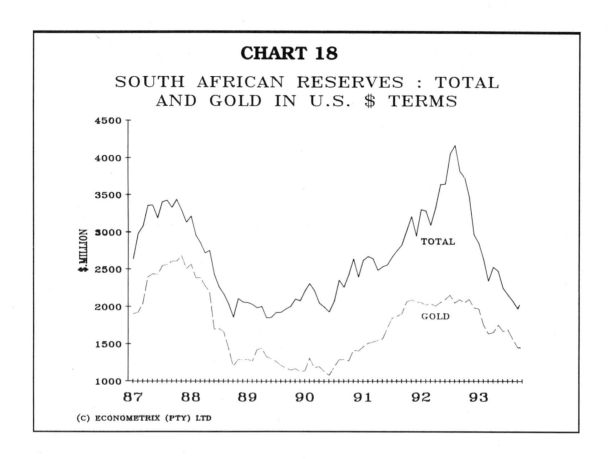

CHART 18

SOUTH AFRICAN RESERVES : TOTAL
AND GOLD IN U.S. $ TERMS

(C) ECONOMETRIX (PTY) LTD

Financing investment

The question to ask is: Do we actually need World Bank loans and other forms of financing? And this question has been thrown open by the ANC in recent weeks, and quite rightly so, because the fact of the matter is — and I'm sure Mr. Tucker will actually elucidate some of these areas — the fact is that there is an awful lot of finance available inside of South Africa.

You can see how the total assets of the private financial institutions has been soaring ahead for over a decade, and yet the level of fixed investment in the country has been collapsing [Chart 20].

Therefore, the question to ask, and the biggest challenge facing the country, is how to convert all this finance that actually exists in the country into real fixed investment.

This is to an extent also a global problem. Even in the United States, you've got a lot of money going into financial institutions, and relatively little of that going into the creation of employment opportunities through fixed investment. But in South Africa, it is a very serious problem.

CHART 19

ESTIMATED FOREIGN DEBT REDEMPTION SCHEDULE ($ BILLIONS)

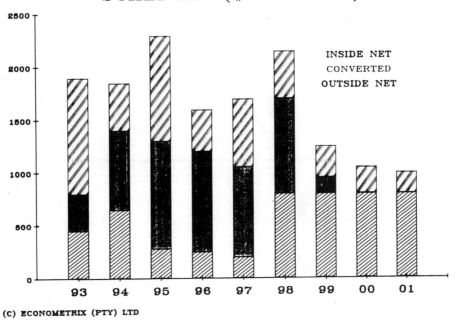

INSIDE NET
CONVERTED
OUTSIDE NET

CHART 20

TOTAL ASSETS OF PRIVATE INSTITUTIONS AS % OF GDP VS GROSS DOMESTIC FIXED INVESTMENT AS % OF GDP

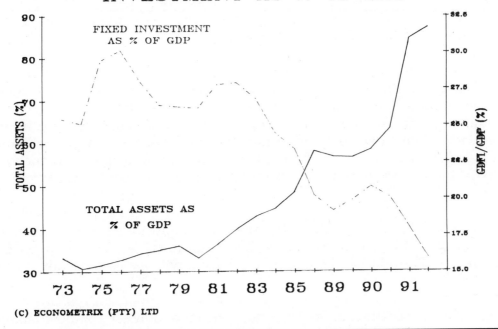

FIXED INVESTMENT
AS % OF GDP

TOTAL ASSETS AS
% OF GDP

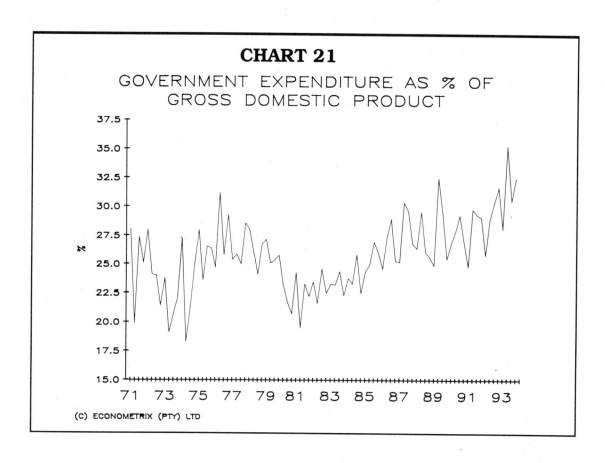

CHART 21

GOVERNMENT EXPENDITURE AS % OF GROSS DOMESTIC PRODUCT

(C) ECONOMETRIX (PTY) LTD

Structural weaknesses

Therefore, I would like to spend the last five minutes in going through what I believe are the fundamental structural weaknesses of the economy that need to be alleviated if we are to convert the short-term, three-year upswing that I think could materialize, into something that will be sustainable.

The first is the need to gradually liberalize our trade and to get rid of protection, which has been with us for several years. We must also get rid of foreign exchange controls and the dual exchange rate system, which have been bottling up liquidity inside the country and leading to more and more concentration of power within the business community, in the hands of fewer and larger organizations. That money is racing after its own tail on the Johannesburg Stock Exchange rather than being invested in the social upliftment of the masses.

Part of the problem is, of course, that there is a political problem in reaching agreement with the people who would benefit from these projects in actually allocating those funds. And I'm sure Mr. Tucker will speak more about that.

The third and probably, in my view, one of the most important reasons for the long-term decline of the economy has been the incredibly sharp and sustained

CHART 22

TOTAL TAXES AS % OF GROSS DOMESTIC PRODUCT

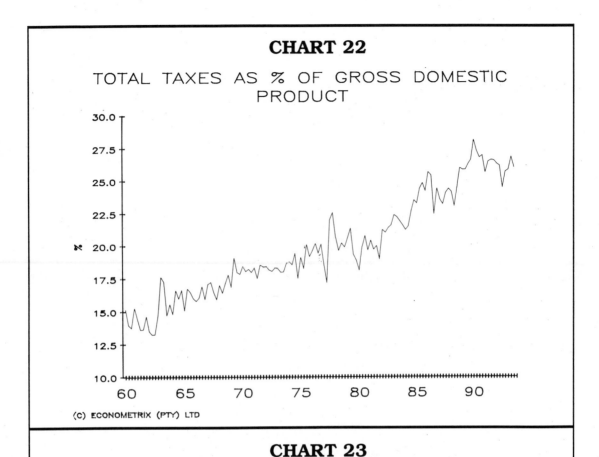

CHART 23

GOVERNMENT CONSUMPTION VS GOVERNMENT INVESTMENT AS % OF GROSS DOMESTIC PRODUCT

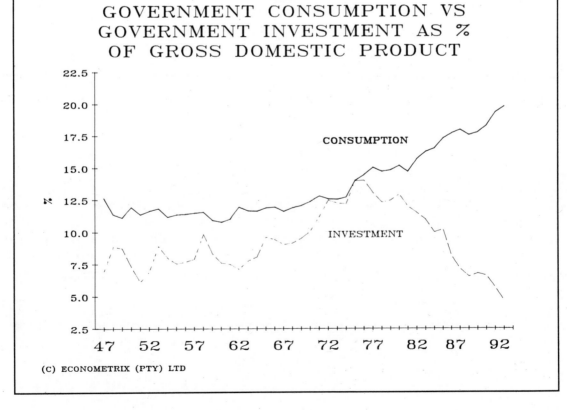

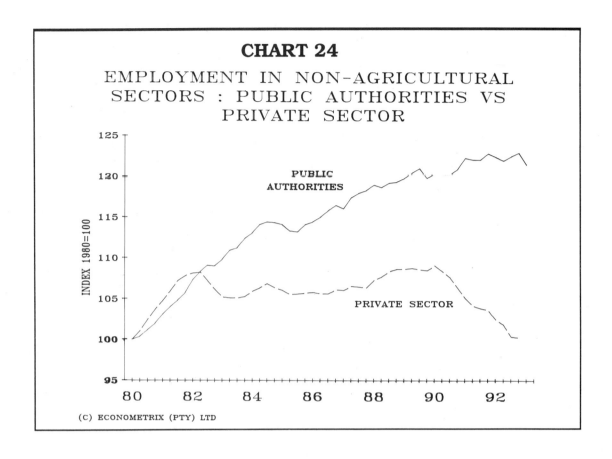

CHART 24

EMPLOYMENT IN NON-AGRICULTURAL
SECTORS : PUBLIC AUTHORITIES VS
PRIVATE SECTOR

(C) ECONOMETRIX (PTY) LTD

increase in government expenditure as a percentage of overall economic activity [Chart 21]. In order to pay for that government spending, taxes have had to be raised consistently [Chart 22]. People have actually become poorer.

What are the causes of this growth in government spending? Unfortunately, the government is not spending on infrastructure—on houses, schools and the like. On the contrary, you can see that, and I believe it is no coincidence that, the economy has been in decline since precisely the point when the government started cutting back on infrastructural spending in order to devote more and more resources on the creation of administrative apartheid structures [Chart 23].

The homelands have involved creating a massive industry of bureaucrats throughout the country. And people have had to be taxed ever more in order to pay for these huge bureaucracies. You can see how public authorities' employment has just kept rising, whereas the private sector has been forced to cut back on employment [Chart 24].

One of the big challenges that we face, one that I don't think is considered or debated sufficiently in South Africa, is how to control the size of the public service. Under a new South Africa with affirmative action programs, the danger

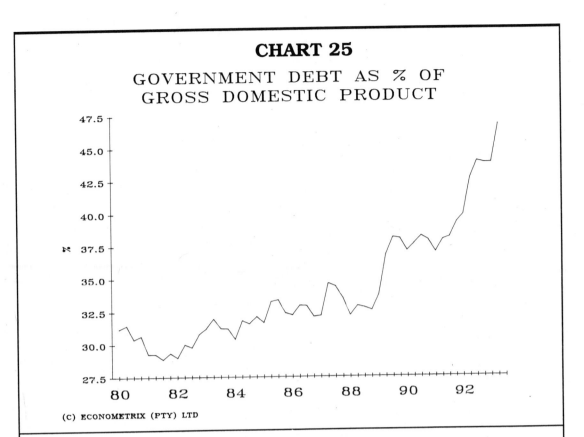

CHART 25

GOVERNMENT DEBT AS % OF GROSS DOMESTIC PRODUCT

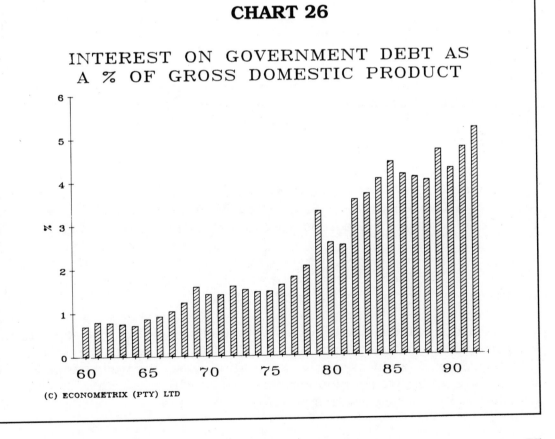

CHART 26

INTEREST ON GOVERNMENT DEBT AS A % OF GROSS DOMESTIC PRODUCT

35

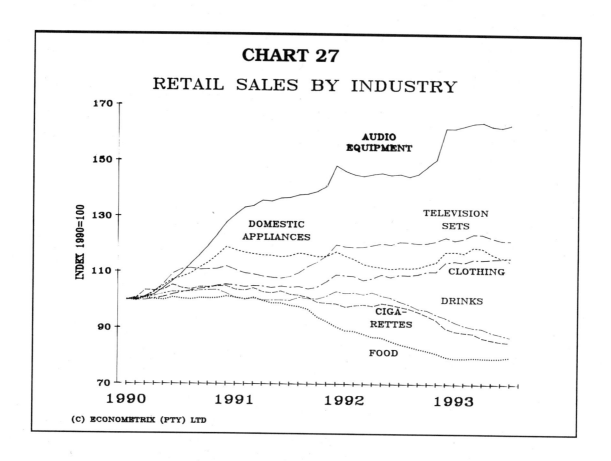

is that the public service will expand even further, requiring taxes to rise still further, and making people poorer as a consequence.

Linked to that, we have the same problem that you Americans have: our budget deficit, in order to pay for government expenditures, has also been expanding. We have a budget deficit now of around 8 percent of GDP, in the face of very, very low growth.

What that is leading to, of course, is an increase in the government's own public debt [Chart 25]. The government not only has to tax more, it has to borrow more and more on capital markets to finance its expenditure. And as the government debt keeps increasing, so, too, does the interest payable on that debt [Chart 26].

Therefore, one of the big challenges we face is how to control the growth of government, and how to redirect government resources into actual social upliftment, rather than into the creation of bureaucracies.

The structural problems don't end there. Another big problem we face is not only the power of big business, which has stifled entrepreneurship and made it very difficult for small businesses to survive, but likewise, the tremendous growth in the power of the trade union movement in South Africa, which is almost a counterbalance to the growth of power in big business.

TABLE 2
WAYS OF FUNDING SOCIAL UPLIFTMENT

- REDUCE GOVERNMENT BUREAUCRACY AND DEFENCE SPENDING

- HIGHER TAXES

- INCREASE PUBLIC DEBT

- PRINT MONEY

- PRESCRIBED ASSET REQUIREMENTS

- PRIVATISATION

- NATIONALISATION

- ECONOMIC GROWTH

As a result, we are seeing some very strange developments now, one of which is the development of a two-tier structure of haves and have-nots no longer along purely racial lines, black and white, but within the black community itself it is remarkable that in the midst of a recession, sales of audio appliances, television sets, clothing and domestic appliances are doing quite well, whereas sales of food, cigarettes and drinks have been falling. In other words, people have been shifting expenditure in the middle of a recession into areas that normally are regarded as discretionary spending, while cutting back on industries involved in essential goods and services [Chart 27].

Part of the explanation is crime; people are replacing appliances that have been stolen. It's also partly a function of the rent boycotts in the townships that have given people more discretionary income.

I think it's also a function of a society in which the trade union members who are employed in the formal sector are doing very well for themselves and their members are able to spend on these appliances, but at the expense of more and more people retrenched from the formal sector, and having to try to eke out a living in the informal sector.

So you've got two million economically active blacks who are gainfully employed in the formal sector and doing well, but more and more people being unemployed and unable even to afford basic foodstuffs.

The need for economic growth

The question to ask is: How are we actually going to fund the growth of upliftment? And this is where I would hope that American influence and experience in developing the educational and training abilities of the black community, and in helping the entrepreneurial spirit truly develop, will succeed in exploiting the remarkable potential that really exists.

Here I have listed a number of ways of funding all the social upliftment, all the conventional ways [Table 2]. But at the end of them all is the most basic manner of all, and that is economic growth. Simply with a 3 percent growth rate for the next five years, the tax base of the country will increase by almost a half, and provide more finance for social upliftment than any form of taxation or nationalization or borrowing could do. The biggest challenge that we face, then, is merely to sustain a bit of growth over a period of time, rather than have these little boom-bust cycles that we've been living with for several decades.

I think the potential is there. I think the potential is absolutely enormous. But first and foremost, we really and truly have to grapple with some of these structural impediments, or else we will not be able to convert what I think will be at least a short-term upswing in 1955-96 into something that can be sustainable and that can uplift all South Africans.

ROBERT S.K. TUCKER

I'm going to start where Azar finished off, which is the need for economic growth. And I am going to make four points.

Economic growth is fundamental

The first point is a very obvious one, which Azar makes, and that is that economic growth is fundamental to South Africa. Just to add a couple of other statistics frequently forgotten, you're actually talking about a $100 billion economy. Last year it contracted by just under 2 percent. In other words, it contracted by $2 billion. That contraction of $2 billion is in actual fact greater than the entire economy of some 30 sub-Saharan economies. To repeat, the contraction in our economy last year was greater than the total economy of some 30 sub-Saharan economies. That will give you an indication of how significant it is.

Conversely, if we had the 3 percent annual growth rate that Azar hopes for, that would be the equivalent of an additional $3 billion per annum. The USAID is represented here, the World Bank's just down the road. If we add all of these guys together, in their wildest dreams they're not going to get close to bringing us $3 billion per annum.

Helping South Africa onto a sustainable and satisfactory growth rate makes a far greater contribution than all the development and aid agencies of the world can actually bring to us. So, it is an indicator of how important it is that we are re-established on a significantly higher and sustainable growth rate. That's point number one.

Severe distortions persist

Point number two is that the structure of the South African economy is very severely distorted.

We started off as a classic colonial economy. The colonialists came to South Africa, where they found a country very rich in minerals and in unskilled labor. They did the natural thing. They applied the unskilled labor to extracting the minerals, and they exported the minerals. And that was absolutely great as long as the world needed primary products.

Robert S.K. Tucker is a director of the law firm of Edward Nathan & Friedland Inc. and chairman of the Community Banking Project, in South Africa.

Of course, over the last several years, there's been a radical shift in what the world needed, and the value of our primary products has declined significantly in relative terms.

But apart from that, as a result of the apartheid system, we inwardly oriented very much more aggressively than would normally be the case. So, for example, we built huge import substitution industries, things like Sasol, Mossgas, Iscor, you name it. Huge amounts of money were invested in what in actual fact, are inwardly oriented, capital-intensive, inefficient industries.

Now, apart from that, we aggravated it by fighting wars against our neighbors, which is not a very intelligent thing to do. You destabilize the markets that you should be trying to market to. We "overspent" $30 billion on defense, which I think is a wonderful way of describing waging wars of destabilization against your neighbors.

The estimate of the cost of completely eliminating the housing backlog for South Africa is only $15 billion. So in other words, we overspent on defense double the cost of eliminating the housing backlog.

So, the economy has got to be fundamentally restructured. Any potential American investor who is interested in investing in the restructuring process, and in developing South Africa's manufacturing capability, should know that South Africa's capacity to develop a manufacturing capability is quite considerable.

Despite the bleak statistics on literacy and technical ability, South Africa in fact is rich in human resources. It is rich in infrastructure. It is a country which has legal systems and so forth with which you are comfortable. So there is enormous potential for the reconstruction of South Africa's economy and its manufacturing capability.

But it must be understood that if you just stick at point number one, in other words, stimulating trade with South Africa as it is presently structured, that has very short-term prospects. It is not sustainable. You must also address point number two, which is the fundamental reconstruction of the South African economy.

Normalize internal capital flows

Which brings me to point number three. Because we have this wonderful economy where a very small and elite group of people, most of whom are white (and as I understand Mamphela, male,) the income discrepancy is 10:1. The GDP per white capita is $6,000 per annum. The GDP per black capita is $600 per annum. This means that the mass of the South African population constitutes a low-income country. That means that you have got to change the capital flows fundamentally.

40

Let me give you a very simple example. The World Bank finds that at our stage of development, we South Africans should be spending 5 percent of GDP on housing—$5 billion per annum. We're actually only spending around about $600 million per annum on housing. And the consequence of it is that we have 1.3 million people who are homeless.

To normalize the capital flow, we would have to spend an extra $4.4 billion per annum on housing. (However, let me say to our USAID friends: I don't want to discourage you from continuing to be involved; I'm going to come to that in a moment.) If you think about what USAID and the World Bank and everyone else can actually bring to the party in terms of housing the South African population, they can't come close to what South Africa itself should be doing.

So we're in this extraordinary predicament. Unlike any other developing country, it has much more to do with the appropriate allocation of South Africa's own resources than it has got to do with what can we get from overseas.

So, point number three is that we've got to normalize our own internal capital flows, which does not detract from the point made by Azar, and I'm in complete agreement with it, that we have also got to be able to become a positive importer of foreign capital for precisely the reasons that Azar explained. And that is that any upturn in economic growth is immediately being cut off as a result of running into balance of payments problems and having to raise interest rates in order to cope with the negative balance of payments.

Strengthen institutional fabric

Point number four is a point which I regret is grossly neglected and ill-analyzed and misunderstood. And that has to do with institutional fabric. Up until the mid-1970s, the conventional wisdom right around the world was that what made a country wealthy was in actual fact its mineral resources and how you optimized the utilization of mineral and agricultural resources of the nation.

And of course, the Japanese totally destroyed that myth, because they had no gold, no coal, no iron, no steel — nothing —and they ran away from the rest of us, demonstrating that in actual fact the wealth of a country is not in its mineral resources and its agricultural capacity. The conventional wisdom has now shifted to the perspective that the wealth of a country is its people, their education, their skills, and their so-called "work ethic."

And I fear that we are not getting to grips with the real issue. We are misidentifying what is cause and what is effect. Because, if we take the United States as an example, when those European immigrants arrived here, the chaps from Ireland and Eastern Europe and so forth, they certainly didn't arrive on the shores of your country as highly educated, highly skilled people.

When de Tocqueville visited this country in 1836, what astounded him was that he found a nation of what he called "joiners." Everyone on these shores was a member of 10, 15 different organizations, of churches, trade organizations, craft unions, welfare organizations and social organizations, and what you had was a rich institutional fabric — something which people were able to engage.

And then of course what happened was that having engaged, the first generation was tremendously frustrated because there was so much they could have done if only they had been better educated. They put pressure on the second generation, sent them to school. The second generation also grew up in an environment without books, without intellectual discourse. Those people also joined, but were equally frustrated because they could have done so much more if they had been better-educated.

They in turn put pressure on the third generation, who now grew up in an environment where there were books and intellectual discourse, and it was really only at the fourth generation that you started to get this incredible surge.

But the *cause* was, in actual fact, the institutional fabric that empowered people and enabled them to achieve their potential because there was a system of relationships where they could engage, interact and produce. Their education and skills development, in actual fact, was consequential, not causative.

Now what has happened in South Africa is that the indigenous Africans had a rich institutional fabric. Their institutional fabric could be described as the carpet on which you are sitting over there, and it was particularly rich in family relationships — very rich family arrangements.

What happened right through the nineteenth century, was that enormous damage was done to that institutional fabric of the indigenous Africans. The damage began with a series of wars waged by Shaka Zulu, which devastated the whole of the eastern seaboard, followed quickly thereafter by the Frontier Wars with the British, followed by the wars with the Boers.

Then we found diamonds and gold. And what happened was the British came in with their bright red carpet. I'd like you to believe that over here where I'm standing is a bright red imperial carpet, representing the rich institutional fabric of big mining houses, financial institutions, their systems of central, regional and local government and so forth.

The introduction of this fabric continued to severely erode the fabric on which you're sitting, the fabric of the indigenous Africans. The introduction of the migratory labor practice, for instance, removed the male head of the household from that African fabric and made him dependent on this fabric over here.

The result is that the indigenous African fabric, over a period of 100 to 150 years, has been in constant deterioration, making them ever more dependent on the institutional fabric where I'm standing.

The tragedy was, those people who now became dependent on this institutional fabric were unable to engage it. This fabric was white, it spoke English and Afrikaans, it was technocratic, it was commercial; while they were black, they spoke Zulu and Xhosa, they were not commercially literate. Although they were dependent on this fabric for their work, their accommodation, everything, they were unable to be empowered by it because they were culturally unable to engage it.

As the twentieth century progressed, however, those people began to engage the enclave institutions and to become empowered by this Western institutional fabric that I described. Then, all of a sudden, in the mid-twentieth century, the development, the empowerment process was cut off stone dead. Why? The apartheid system said, "Terribly sorry; you guys who live there, even if you are now able to engage this fabric, we're going to prohibit you from rising to the level of a supervisor. Even if you have now learned how to talk to the banks, we're going to prohibit you from borrowing money for the purposes of home owner-ship; we're going to prohibit you from borrowing money for the purposes of establishing business." And so we carried on for *another* 40 years.

And now the tragedy, the thing that is really frustrating the reconstruction and the development of our country, is the devastation of the indigenous fabric and the dependence of those people on this Western fabric, which comes back to what Mamphela was talking about. That is, it is not only a question of the transformation of this Western, white fabric so that it is empowering of those people, but also of the development of institutional capacity, the institutional fabric, within the African community. Unless you do that, you can't bring about development.

Let me just give you two very simple examples. The Development Bank of South Africa last year had R1 billion to invest. They only managed to invest R440 million. That is not because of incompetence; it is not because they lack dedication. They are dedicated and competent people. Why could they only manage to invest R440 million out of the R1 billion available to them? The answer is the absence of institutions which serve the mass of the people.

Another example is the IDT [Independent Development Trust] Finance Corpo-ration, which was established two-and-a-half years ago with R300 million. It's earned another R60 million in interest and yet, it has only managed to lend R60 million. Why? It is not because of incompetence. It is because of the lack of the fabric, of the capacity, to actually deliver development into the community.

Now, that is point number four. But we can't have any conditionality placed on investment. I am totally supportive of the call which was made last week for the unconditional lifting of sanctions.

We go back to points one and two, which is to stimulate the economy and to reconstruct. You cannot do that if you're going to impose conditionality. But what we do need is a high level of understanding by all people who are genuinely interested in the future of our country of points three and four. The capital flows within the country have got to be normalized and South Africa has got to use its own resources for the benefit of the entire South African community. Secondly, this issue of institutional fabric is absolutely crucial. There is no prospect of sustainable prosperity for any of us in South Africa unless we develop institutions and institutional arrangements which empower all of the people of our country.

JOHN LAMOLA

The call for the lifting of economic sanctions against South Africa was finally made on September 24, 1993, in Mr. Mandela's historic address to the United Nations.

Acting upon his concern at the strains on the South African economy presently, the ANC has backed this call with a campaign to boost foreign investment and to market South Africa to the international investor community. However, in initiating this new framework of the ANC's international strategy, Mr. Mandela reckoned, "We must warn that we are not yet out of the woods."

The purpose of my short presentation is to amplify this expression. We—the churches—wish to draw attention to what we consider to be the pressing realities that need to be faced in South Africa as it enters this new dispensation of being considered as a potential destination of foreign investment.

Over and above the presentation of South Africa as an attractive field of investment, we wish to sound two cautions. First, the South African economy that a post-sanctions regime will inherit is still structurally defective. That has been explained by two previous speakers. Moreover, the economy is a morally problematic edifice of apartheid that awaits fundamental restructuring.

As corollary to the foregoing, our second warning is that a failure to recognize this will lead to conditions that will exacerbate socio-political instability, which already is a major factor mitigating against a positive investment environment in South Africa.

The process of political change now underway, much as it has brought commendable advances in converting South Africa from a racial oligarchy to a non- racial democracy, does not give absolute assurance that in the medium-term this political process alone can deliver peace, quiet and prosperity to all South Africans. The forces of democracy, as led by the African National Congress, may not have adequate political power to timely address the legacies of apartheid, and thereby preempt the expected disillusionment of the poor masses, which may express itself in political unrest.

In the light of this, our proposal would be that this conjuncture, with an economy awaiting reform, the prospects of a weak government and the potential

---

John Lamola, a private consultant, coordinates the Task Force on Economic Matters of the South African Council of Churches.

of growing social discontent among the economically marginalized, necessitates the introduction of a social responsibility program aimed at redressing the economic legacy of injustice of the apartheid system.

All this, we argue, justifies the introduction of the [South African Council of Churches] Code of Corporate Conduct, which will serve as an interventional mechanism in the interim before the full realization of a restructured economy.

But let me further illustrate the problem. As we emerge into the post-sanctions era and face the end of the twentieth century, South Africa faces two acute and urgent needs which are interrelated.

The imperative of economic justice

The first one is the need to catapult the economy onto a growth path that would get the country out of the current recession, and enable the socio-economic legacies of apartheid affecting the black majority to be addressed effectively and timeously. It is generally accepted that this can be achieved through a phenomenal rise in levels of investment, in particular, foreign investment.

The second need is that of economic justice, or rather, the installation of political mechanisms and frameworks that will ensure a fair achievement of this justice in good time. Time is of the essence here.

The political changes that have ensued since 1990 have in a way been successful primarily in suspending political repression by the state. Paradoxically, as this political liberalization wears on, the economic configuration is emerging as the arena with immense potential for political conflict and consequent social instability. The need to address and pre-empt this political instability, which could threaten economic revival at a time when it is most needed, is the foremost challenge to leaders of all sectors of South African civil society.

There is going to be no political stability in South Africa if there is not going to be a concerted effort at responding to the economic grievances of the poor, the alienated black majority and workers. If business and the new democratic government are not going to work together on instituting a systematic program to redress the social injustices fostered by apartheid, South Africa's future will be characterized by endless conflict, unrest and social disintegration.

In the latest draft of what has been called the "Reconstruction and Development Program," which has gone through the African National Congress's Executive Committee, and was presented to the recent Special Congress of the Congress of South African Trade Unions, we are aptly warned by COSATU, "An election victory by the ANC alliance is imperative. But an election victory is only a first step. No political democracy can survive and flourish if the mass of our people remain in poverty without jobs, without land, without tangible prospects for a better life."

46

Therefore, we need economic revival and growth. We need economic justice. We need massive foreign investment. And the question is: Can these three imperatives be balanced or be reconciled?

Political realities

To further illustrate this, one may go into the structural problems of the apartheid economy. My two colleagues have already addressed that. But what I wish to focus on in the next five minutes is the question of the political realities.

Yes, the Transitional Executive Council will have a subcouncil on finance, which will effectively assume powers to effect and monitor transitional economic policy. But this TEC mechanism will be composed of a group of political parties who represent a plethora of irreconcilable agendas and interests. From the perception of the grassroots communities, between now and the time of elections, that is, during the time of the rule of the TEC, it will require continued struggle and a substantial political will on their part to ensure that the TEC makes decisive macroeconomic changes in the short-term.

The structural distortion described earlier are essentially what this subcouncil on finance organized by the TEC is inheriting, and what the international business community is invited to participate in now that sanctions have been repealed.

The greatest task and challenge of the TEC will be to change this scenario as soon as possible so as to make South Africa a viable investment option. To achieve this, however, will require tremendous political will and power and management.

The urge for a timeously negotiated political settlement has meant that the cardinal dynamic of the current negotiations between the liberation organizations and forces of the apartheid status quo has been compromise. There have been major compromises from all sides of the negotiations table. The full import of this compromise is still to manifest itself in the kind of South Africa that will result from the whole process, and it is still unclear whether the people in this majority will accept that compromise-crafted South Africa.

It is also important to note that the primary goal of the democratic elections scheduled for April 1994 is not to constitute a new government in the sense of the installation of a permanent constitutional dispensation. What will be elected is an "interim government of national unity," which will govern on the basis of an interim constitution.

The primary assignment of this government will be to oversee the production of the final constitution, which the 400 elected delegates will be debating in the constituent assembly. This process, of writing a final constitution, is expected to last nine months to two years from April 1994. In other words, what you are facing is only, to some extent, the institutionalization of the negotiations, which have been going on and off since September 1991.

The social and political stresses which accompany political horse trading and which South Africans have endured since early 1990, will therefore continue at least until the middle of 1995.

Overseeing this grand organ of constitutional negotiations, and responsible for governing the country, will be a cabinet constituted on a proportional basis by representatives from all of the parties that obtain 5 percent or more of the vote in the general election.

The politics of coalition governance dictate that such a government will of necessity have a weak and slow policy-making drive. Therefore, this post-April 1994 government may not be able to respond with the required expediency to the social crisis described earlier. The historic expectation of the black majority for an immediate eradication of all the vestiges of apartheid is bound for a devastating frustration.

Besides the political paralysis resulting from having to balance the conflicting interests of the various social groups, this new government will have to deal with the reality that even under the best of scenarios, the South African economy can only be expected to experience an annual GDP growth of 2.5 percent — my two colleagues have talked of 3 percent — from the middle of April 1994.

Considering the depreciation dating from 1985, and what Mr. Tucker has just said about the economy's shrinkage of 2 percent, a growth rate of 2.5 or 3 percent experienced from the middle of 1994 will in effect mean that the South African economy will only be 1 percent bigger in 1995 that it was in 1985.

Based on these calculations, experts in social spending policy predict that it will take at least 10 years to achieve parity in the quality of education and health services offered to black communities and their white counterparts.

Under these circumstances, a rapid disenchantment of the black masses and possible revolt cannot be ruled out. This completes the vicious circle of economic depression, political unrest and instability, further depression as domestic and foreign investment is scared away, ad infinitum.

The need for a code of conduct

What is to be done? It is on the basis of this analysis, perspective and deep concern that the South African Council of Churches has over the past two years actively advocated an institution of instruments of ethical economic activity that will signal to the masses of South Africans that the future government and business intend to promote economic justice.

This has culminated in the production of a Code of Conduct for business operating in South Africa. The general criticism we have had to deal with is that South Africa cannot afford such a code; that economic recession is so bad that South Africa must in the short-term do with any kind of capital investment it can get; that the code makes the country unattractive as a destination of foreign investment. To this we have responded that given the scenario and the analysis that I have just presented, South Africa needs some codified commitment to socially responsible business practice more than anything else. By subscribing to a code of some form, business will be registering its intent to see all the negative effects of apartheid eradicated. In this way, where it could serve as a medium of delivering justice at the economic plane, the Code can be an instrument of political stability.

For economic growth in the shortest possible term, South Africa needs socio-political stability. It needs a social contract between business, the black communities which business serves, the workers and the nascent democratic government. The only form of such a contract under the present circumstances is a code of conduct, which states the responsibilities of business towards these sectors, and in turn puts these sectors in common effort with business for responsible economic growth.

In the light of this, if the *conditio sine qua non* of economic growth is political stability, the *conditio sine qua non* of political stability in South Africa is a code of conduct for business.

How the code will work

An encouraging number of business leaders in South Africa have appreciated the need of such a code and engaged us in very constructive criticism and debate. This has led us to the establishment of the following as the fundamental principles that are to govern the promotion and implementation of this code.

One, we understand that business does not carry all the responsibility for the evils of apartheid, and cannot be expected to bear single-handedly the task of eradicating all that apartheid has done. Therefore, this code is not a panacea for the economic ills of South Africa, not does it preclude related macroeconomic restructuring that needs to be undertaken so as to improve the business environment in South Africa.

Two, it applies to both South African and foreign companies of all sizes.

Three, the code is voluntary. It is not intended to be enforced by legislation of any government, now or in the future. However, a democratic government will be expected to translate the standards promoted in the code into components of its positive investment policy.

Fourth, the promotion and implementation of the code must be and will be a collective task involving business and other sectors of civil society in South Africa, such as the labor movement, community civic organizations, and religious communities.

Business, we believe, must be involved in the formulation of the implementation-cum-monitoring system of the code.

Finally, the spirit of this code as well as the system for its implementation shall be exhortational. It will represent a call to business in South Africa to programmatically strive at all times and in all its operations for socially responsible practices. For this reason, the implementation processes shall, methodologically, be an assessment of the growth or otherwise of corporate social responsibility in South Africa.

In inclusion, those who see nothing wrong with the social status quo in South Africa will not see the need for an instrument to encourage an ethical business practice at the microeconomic level and a socially responsible investment regime at the macroeconomic level.

Being a means of assuaging the frustrations of the victims of the economic ravages of apartheid, a code is a preventive instrument for peace. Without a mechanism for the promotion of ethically sensitive economic activity, such as the code promoted by the SACC, the future democratic government has no option but to prepare itself to deal with the uprisings of the poor, which will need Draconian and violent means to suppress.

The vicious circle which I have described of economic depression and instability can be broken and converted into a virtuous circle of cooperation between business, the people, and the democratic government.

THE U.S. COMMERCE DEPARTMENT AND THE NEW SOUTH AFRICA

RONALD H. BROWN

These are exciting times, not only in America but all around the world. I know many in this room have been waiting for this day, have wondered whether in our lifetimes we would see the announcements that have been made recently, and are overwhelmed that we have. Now, we have to figure out how to respond to it in a way that really makes sense.

I would like to thank the Investor Responsibility Research Center for putting on this extremely important conference, and thank all of the participants for their interest in ensuring long term economic growth in post-apartheid South Africa—an important mission for us to embark on. Working for an end to apartheid has been a personal commitment of mine and, I know, a personal commitment of many of you, for an awfully long time. We're clearly exhilarated by the events of the last month: the Sept. 23 action by the South African parliament to create the Transitional Executive Council giving the majority of South Africans a first ever role in governing their country, obviously a watershed event; and passage the same day of laws creating independent media and electoral commissions in anticipation of the April 27 (1994) multiparty elections—another crucial step; and the call by Mr. Mandela for the lifting of remaining international economic sanctions against South Africa during his Sept. 24 address to the United Nations, another incredibly important event in this process.

Supporting economic development in South Africa

This Administration supports strong commercial and business ties in a post-apartheid South Africa between the United States and South Africa. As the President has stated, "Removing sanctions is not enough. Americans who have been so active in breaking down the pillars of apartheid must remain committed to helping build the non-racial, market democracy that comes in its wake." I know that is a view we all share. As we talk about building a non-racial society, as we talk about democracy, as we talk about market-driven economies, we are led unalterably to this conclusion: none of it makes a whole lot of difference in the everyday life of people unless we can foster economic development and create high wage, high quality jobs for the majority of the people of South Africa. And that is what we are committed as a government to helping to do. We expect that with the establishment of the TEC, we will no longer block International Monetary Fund lending to South Africa. We will offer investment guarantees to

Ronald H. Brown is the U.S. Secretary of Commerce.

53

encourage American commercial involvement, and we will foster trade by opening negotiations on a bilateral tax treaty.

To further confirm the Administration's commitment to strong economic growth in South Africa, President Clinton has asked me to lead the first trade and commercial mission to South Africa. I am obviously honored to have that responsibility. I can think of no more exciting mission that the President can ask me to undertake. I had the opportunity to spend some time with Mr Mandela a week ago Saturday, when he was in Washington, and he shares the excitement that President Clinton and I both have about this mission. We are planning it now. We believe that we will do it towards the end of November and spend somewhere between three and six days in South Africa.

The President has also asked me to focus on the black South African business community and how we can create an environment for enterpreneurship and economic development among black enterpreneurs who obviously have been very inhibited in their ability to pursue their economic dreams in the past. But I have also had the opportunity, even before the mission takes place, to speak to a number of white South African business leaders about how we can work together and to pull in the same direction through joint ventures and other kinds of business relationships to foster the kind of economic growth and development that both the United States and the new South Africa seek.

Assisting U.S. business in South Africa

Developing bilateral commercial interests between the United States and South Africa is clearly a major focus of the Department of Commerce. In addition to the commercial trade mission, we hope to increase our resources in the Southern Africa region to ensure that U.S. businesses get the assistance they need to expand commercial and trade ties with South Africa and throughout the region. Currently, the Commerce Department's U.S. foreign and commercial service has commercial offices in both Johannesburg and Cape Town, and we really want to expand that activity so that we can be a vehicle for the American business community to reach out and solidify the kind of commercial relationships that they seek.

There is absolutely no question that American business has a crucial role to play in contributing to South Africa's post-apartheid economic development and to the development of a non-racial market democracy. Enabling and expanding U.S. commercial and trade ties can promote real economic and social opportunity for the newly emerging black private sector.

African-Americans, I believe, also have a special role to play in this regard. Much of the impetus for the struggle to end apartheid has come from the American black community. We cannot forget that leadership. A number of African-American enterpreneurs and leaders want to be involved in this effort to ensure economic development in South Africa and in the entire region of Africa. We want to make sure that we reach out to them as well.

President Clinton and I recently announced the lauching of a new national export strategy for America. I think we all recognize, particularly those in the business community, that exports might well be the key to our economic future. Every billion dollar increase in exports means 20,000 new jobs for the American people. And if you look at our economic performance over the last several years of recession and stagnation, and now with the most modest of recoveries and in some places in America no recovery at all, one of the few bright spots has been exports. But our judgment is that we have only just scratched the surface on encouraging exports, particularly on getting small and medium-sized businesses and minority and women-owned businesses into the export market-place. We have got to focus on those kinds of opportunities, and we intend to do that.

We have made some rather dramatic efforts over the last couple of weeks. Basically, by decisions we made at the Commerce Department level through my chairmanship of the Trade Promotion Co-ordinating Committee, we freed about $35 billion of U.S. exports by a stroke of the pen. We have set a goal for American exports to be at the $1 trillion level by the turn of the century. If we meet that, which I think we will, that means the creation of six million more jobs for the American people. So, thinking about exports is really a serious way of thinking about sustained economic growth in America. Clearly that is one of the very practical reasons why we want to look at this new market place for American products and develop the kind of relationship that we need. But it is a two-way street.

We see that clearly in the interest of the United States to support economic growth and economic development with our brothers and sisters in South Africa. I am absolutely confident that the American business community will respond enthusiastically to the new challenge of pursuing commercial opportunities in South Africa. South Africa's $20 billion import market is crucial not only to the continent of Africa, but to ourselves. We are going to be more and more reliant on the the ability of developing countries to purchase American products, so we should focus on the significant economic opportunities that we have. Clearly the emergence of South Africa as a regional gateway is terribly important.

A more dynamic U.S. government role

We are clearly fortunate to live in a time of emerging freedom and opportunity around the world. It is a very exciting, very challenging time. Since our own national security is inextricably tied to our economic security, it means that we have got to change the way we think in this very complicated and difficult international economic environment in which we now have to function. Clearly, we have to use this opportunity of great global change to redefine the relationship between the public and private sector in America into a new kind of partnership. I believe we have wasted 30 years in a ridiculous debate about what is the role of government, while our commercial competitors decided that a long time ago. And they are just knocking our socks off all around the world because we are still trying to figure it out. There are times when government just needs to get out of the way; there are other times when government can be a better and more effective partner. We are dedicated and committed to being a better and more effective partner with, but also a strong advocate for, American business and industry.

When you look around the world and you see President Mitterand and Chancellor Kohl and Prime Minister Major jumping on airplanes to fly to distant corners of the world to support the interests of French, German or British business and industry, you wonder why we in America do not do the same thing. Well, we are going to be doing the same thing. We would like to think that our start was a trip I took to Saudi Arabia about three months ago. People said: "Why are you going to Saudi Arabia?" I said, "I am going to Saudi Arabia because the king is about to make a decision on $10 billion of contracts, and we would sure like him to pick American companies rather then British or Asian companies." And we are going to maintain that kind of aggressive attitude of working arm in arm, shoulder to shoulder with American business and industry. And that goes for our relationship with South Africa as well.

I deeply appreciate the opportunity to come over and have a few moments to talk with you. I look forward to a continuing dialogue in the future. I know we share the same vision, the same hopes and dreams, the same sense of commitment to making the most that we possibly can of this historic opportunity in South Africa. So I congratulate you on what you have done in the past, and what we will do together in the future.

DEVELOPING BLACK BUSINESSES
AND MANAGERS IN SOUTH AFRICA

DAVID ROBB CRALLE

I'm here to tell you a little bit about the Overseas Private Investment Corporation—What we do in the realm of business development for American investors overseas as well as the specific topic today, which is developing black partners in South Africa.

The first thing you should know about OPIC is that we don't sell oil. It's actually O-P-I-C, not O-P-E-C. It stands for the Overseas Private Investment Corporation, and despite its name, we are actually a U.S. government agency.

OPIC offers a series of financial services to American companies who want to invest overseas. We currently operate in about 150 countries around the world. One notable exception is South Africa. We are in the process of rectifying that situation; we will be negotiating a bilateral agreement, or a government-to-government agreement, between OPIC and the incoming government of South Africa to establish the legal framework under which OPIC will be able to offer its series of financial services and incentives to American companies who would like to invest in South Africa.

Specifically, we have two major programs: One is a program of what's known collectively as Political Risk Insurance. Essentially, this is U.S. government insurance against specific and defined political risks. We also have a Finance Program, that is to say, direct loans and loan guarantees offered for, in its best case, nonrecourse project finance. I should mention that the difference between the services that OPIC offers and the services offered by, for instance, the Export/Import Bank or the U.S. Department of Commerce, is that OPIC is always concentrated on the development of U.S. private sector investment. The Export/Import Bank is primarily concerned with U.S. export trade transactions, and OPIC is concerned with U.S. investment transactions.

Political risk insurance

Essentially, political risk insurance is three defined coverages, and although I am new to Africa and new to South Africa in particular, from everything that I have read and heard in speeches, the three types of political risk insurance coverages that we offer are exactly the kinds of things that the new majority government of South Africa would like to send a message to the investor community not to be worried about. Specifically: We offer insurance against

---

David Robb Cralle is the manager of investment development for Africa at the U.S. Overseas Private Investment Corp.

the inconvertibility of currency; we offer insurance against expropriation; we offer insurance against political violence.

Throughout the re-engagement of U.S. direct foreign investment for productive purposes in South Africa, these are three topics that all U.S. investors will be looking to deal with. And one of the ways that the U.S. government has to assuage these risks is through OPIC political risk insurance coverage.

Through our inconvertibility coverage, we offer insurance against situations where it becomes impossible to convert and remit dividends and profits or to repatriate capital back or out of South Africa. This will be a very important coverage, we suspect, for American companies looking to re-engage themselves in South Africa.

We also offer insurance against the expropriation or nationalization of assets, the taking or the denial of the fundamental rights of the investor to own and to operate a project.

The third kind of insurance is against political violence. That is to say that if there is a project whose *assets* are directly damaged due to political violence, there is compensation. There is also a rider, or an additional type of insurance that is available against loss of *income* directly due to political violence. If, for example, you have a factory with a rail spur into the project, and there is an act of political violence against the rail spur, the actual damage to insured assets can be quite small; whereas the loss of income as a direct result of political violence can be quite large. So, in fact, we offer two types of insurance: One to cover losses to assets, and one to cover loss of income.

Finance assistance

We also offer a finance product. These are direct loans and loan guarantees which, in their best case, are nonrecourse project finance. This is not funding specifically to assist with U.S. exports, although the proceeds of dollar-based lending, obviously, can be used to pay for U.S. exports. Essentially, this is where OPIC will lend or guarantee funds sourced in the American capital markets for the project itself. We look to the cash flows of the project for repayment. We underwrite our loans and loan guarantees just like any commercial bank would, and we offer rates that are market rates. That is to say, the interest rates are not subsidized. Where we are different from commercial lending is that we will take chances; we'll lend in places or under circumstance where commercial banks basically would not.

Other investment services

Now, in the investment development department, we also offer a number of fee investment services, and we have one major program that is in the process now of being put in place. We have recently concluded an agreement with the U.S.

Agency for International Development to sponsor a series of investment missions to South Africa for American companies. In particular, we are working with USAID's Office of Operations and New Initiatives.

We're looking to put on our first investment mission to South Africa in February of 1994. Essentially, it will be a matchmaker operation, and this is why, in fact, I'm on this panel. We would like to identify American companies who are new to South Africa, and take them to South Africa to look at investing there and to introduce them to black businesses who are ready to receive that investment. We will be working through USAID's program called BICSN, the Black Integrated Commercial Support Network, already in South Africa, and this will support a number of other initiatives that USAID already has in place in South Africa to support the majority entrepreneur.

There are a number of sectors that we would like to recruit from, including franchising, infrastructure, agri-business, consumer mass markets, value-added services, information technology, including hardware and software, and financial services, telecommunications — you name it. We are interested in taking new-to-market companies to South Africa to introduce them to majority businesses there.

We have another aspect to our agreement with USAID, which is to fund a project development program, a cost-sharing feasibility studies fund that will be focused in South Africa on the development of black entrepreneurs or joint ventures between American companies and the black majority in South Africa.

In closing, I would just like to acknowledge and thank USAID in particular for going into partnership with us to complete this kind of activity. The Office of Operations and New Initiatives under the leadership of Bill Kaschak has been instrumental in putting this together, and we thank them very much.

ISRAEL B. SKOSANA

Thank you, Chairperson, ladies and gentlemen.

Let me start by thanking IRRC for enabling us to be here today and to share with you some ideas insofar as the South African situation is concerned.

The obstacles facing black entrepreneurs

Ladies and gentlemen, we have heard the previous speakers this morning discussing the issues in South Africa; we've heard from Dr. Ramphele about the violence that is engulfing our country. Unfortunately, there is another kind of silent violence that is really killing our people: the violence of hunger, the violence of poverty, the violence of disease. I am highlighting some of these issues, ladies and gentlemen, because I believe it's important for you to understand the context within which black business operates in South Africa, and also the context from where this black business originates.

Our problems are exacerbated by the very high unemployment rate in my country. Approximately 50 percent of the economically active people are actually unemployed; and, unfortunately, the bulk of those people are from the black community. Bob Tucker referred earlier on to the discrepancy between the ten-to-one distribution of income among the population groups in South Africa. To be precise, whites get about 9.5 rands of income to every one rand of income that blacks receive.

Another problem that we black businesses face is the vast concentration of wealth among a few people. As I'm talking to you now, over 80 percent of the capitalization of the companies on the Johannesburg Stock Exchange is owned by only four conglomerates. And, unfortunately, of those four conglomerates, there is not a single black company. So you can already see that there is a massive discrepancy, yet we are told that we must continue business as normal. My contention is that we cannot, if we are looking for this prosperity for the future of South Africa, afford to continue business as normal. We need to redress some of these imbalances of the past.

Black business today in South Africa contributes less than 2 percent towards the gross domestic product. And if we blacks in the country are really the indigenous people, I believe it's important for us to play a more active role so as

---

Israel B. Skosana is executive director of National Sorghum Breweries Ltd.

to make a bigger contribution towards the GDP rather than this meager 2 percent.

The blame for this situation is on apartheid. One doesn't want to go through all the abhorrences of apartheid, but we know from the business point of view that one of the fundamentals of running a business is to have adequate cash and resources, and that cash can be raised by collateralizing one's property. In South Africa, ladies and gentlemen, you all know that blacks were prohibited from owning land, which is the very asset that the white community uses to collateralize to raise funding for their businesses. It was only in 1984 that blacks were allowed to own property and then only in those so-called townships designated for blacks. Only very recently have the so-called white areas opened up. For all intents and purposes, our hands have been tied in acquiring those means that could enable us to play an active role within the economic arena of South Africa.

Ladies and gentlemen, again I believe it's important for you to know that it was only in 1978 that blacks were allowed to form companies. Before then, as a black person you couldn't operate as a company. Only in 1979 were blacks allowed to form manufacturing companies. No wonder we have hardly any representation in that sector of our country.

The next session, I'm sure, will deal with the issue of management, but I think it's imperative also for me to highlight here that, as I'm talking to you now at this point in time, the black representation on the management of corporate South Africa is a meager 1 to 3 percent, depending on which organization's research you read.

The latest development in my country is whereby blacks are invited to serve on the boards of directors of some of these companies. But if you look at the internal structure of these companies, very little has actually been done to give senior positions to the black people. They don't have black executive directors; those are the directors who have a specific responsibility for the daily running of the business.

The role of the informal sector: Those are the situations, ladies and gentlemen, that I believe we need to address if we are really serious about true freedom, because if we do not address those issues, I'm afraid we are still merely playing. The tendency insofar as black business is concerned is that we are in the "informal" sector. The informal sector is so glorified in my country; in fact, black business today is synonymous with informal sector. It would even appear that there's a deliberate ploy—the way we are seeing it as black people—by the government of the day and even by South African corporations — to make sure that blacks are on the periphery of the economy. When it comes to participating in the mainstream, black people don't get that kind of support.

I'm not suggesting that the informal sector, ladies and gentlemen, is not important. I'm proud of the organization that I'm still involved with, the Get Ahead Foundation, which is playing a very leading role in the informal sector. But I can tell you now that Get Ahead's own research found that the blacks operating in the informal sector do so purely for survival purposes. When we asked them whether, if they were offered a job, they would accept and join that particular company and leave what they are doing, they respond in the positive. The answer is yes.

Therefore, if you read in the papers about this giant informal sector, I think you need to take that kind of opinion with a pinch of salt. We, as black people, want to see ourselves on the mainstream economy of the country, we want to see ourselves in the manufacturing companies, we want to see ourselves running these big organizations and financial institutions, if indeed we are going to have the kind of peace we're talking about.

The need for affirmative action: This brings me, ladies and gentlemen, to the whole issue of affirmative action. I believe affirmative action can address some of these imbalances of the past. I don't want to get into the semantics as to whether it is strategy or policy. I want to stress in South Africa we are talking about the black majority, not the black minority. If we want to redress the imbalances of the past, if, indeed, we want to take all the black community into this new South Africa, affirmative action has to be put in place.

We are all supportive of these unconditional invitations to overseas companies to come and invest in South Africa. But I must say that from the black perspective there is a concern indeed, because we are seeing the status quo being perpetuated. The experience thus far is that the companies coming in are dealing with the very "haves" who have used the apartheid system to prosper. So, as black people, we believe that the codes of conduct under discussion for business in South Africa need to be enforced.

I haven't had time to discuss with Reverend Lamola my view that if you make something non-compulsory, very few people are going to comply with it. As I have indicated to you, some of the companies that are well known for standing up on platforms and saying that they condemn apartheid have done little to advance black managers to senior levels in their companies. With regard to affirmative action, allow me to quote Dr. Mandela: "Affirmative action is not a threat either to standards or to individuals; it's an internationally recognized method of redressing the past wrongs." I strongly believe in this message of Dr. Mandela; we need to take actions in addressing these issues.

National Sorghum Breweries

We have a company called National Sorghum Breweries Ltd. which is actively involved in the whole area of affirmative action. It's a company that believes very strongly in black economic empowerment. National Sorghum Breweries is the

```
┌─────────────────────────────────────────────────────────────┐
│                      NSB's MISSION                            │
│                                                               │
│                                                               │
│   National Sorghum Breweries' mission is black economic empow-│
│   erment through the ownership, control and management of a   │
│   group of companies in the beverage, food and leisure industries.│
│                                                               │
│   We aim at an affirmative action-based policy of employment, │
│   procurement of supplies and services in our business undertak-│
│   ings. This should clearly not be misconstrued as discrimination│
│   in reverse since it is aimed at creating a fair and just society.│
│                                                               │
│   Together we commit ourselves to maintain our leading position in│
│   the industries in which we operate by dedicating ourselves to│
│   fulfilling our customers' needs through excellence of products and│
│   services and to engender a spirit of interdependence between all│
│   parties concerned in our Company to their mutual benefit.   │
│                                                               │
└─────────────────────────────────────────────────────────────┘
```

largest black-owned — and *black-managed* — company in the history of South Africa. This company has been successful over the past three years since its formation. In fact, it's a company that was formed many years ago, but the new structure, where it's got black managment, has only been in existence for three years. And, indeed, we managed to prove to the skeptics out there that if you give the black community an opportunity, it will be in a position of delivering. Our mission at National Sorghum Breweries is black economic empowerment through ownership and management of companies in the beverage, food and leisure industries.

We are at pains, ladies and gentlemen, again to explain that we aim at affirmative action in our employment policy and in the procurement of supplies and services. I say we are at pains because this whole concept of affirmative action is actually misunderstood. We at NSB discuss our affirmative action statement because we regard the whole issue of black economic empowerment as of national interest. For us to pull the black community out of this morass of negative thinking that blacks can't do things on their own, and similarly to pull the white community from the kind of thinking that there is nothing positive that blacks can do, we have to specifically highlight the issue of black economic empowerment.

The majority of the board of directors is black. We are not a racist company; we do have whites in our midst. One director, Peter Wrighton, is a leading industrialist; he is also white. He is the chief executive of Premier, one of the most progressive companies in South Africa. We have again from the white community Dr. Tienie van Vuuren, a leading industrialist and a specialist in

NBB's BOARD OF DIRECTORS

Professor Mohale Mahanyele	Executive Chairman and Chief Executive - (Black)
Israel Skosana	Executive Director - (Black)
Peter Wrighton	Leading industrialist - (White)
Mosce Leoka	Leading advertising specialist - (Black)
Dr. Ndumiso Mzamane	Leading medical specialist
Dr. Mirriam Makeba	Internationally acclaimed singer - (Black)
Lekgau Mathabathe	Leading businessman and educationist - (Black)
Eugene van Rensburg	Financial expert - (White)
Horace Masimula	Leading food retailer - (Black)
Professor Khabi Mngoma	Authority on African music and culture (Black)
Dr. Tienie van Vuuren	Leading industrialist and a specialist in business education - (White)

business education. One of the conditions of participation on our board is to agree and subscribe to this philosophy of black economic empowerment. If U.S. companies want to get involved in South Africa, they should emulate what National Sorghum Breweries is doing. If you look at our board of directors, it reflects the demography of the country, and I believe this is the route that most companies need to take.

The company top management, is basically 98 percent black. We've got a total staff employment of 4,000 people, 95 percent of whom are black.

National Sorghum Breweries has 10,000 shareholders. That is the largest shareholding in the history of South Africa. Business people would know that to have that kind of a shareholding is very expensive, because you got to maintain a register of shareholders and so on. But we did this deliberately because we wanted to enable the ordinary person to be a shareholder in our company. And we are very proud of this approach.

National Sorghum Breweries, ladies and gentlemen, is not listed on a stock exchange. Had we gone to the stock exchange, our company today would be in the hands of some of these conglomerates I spoke about before, and blacks wouldn't have anything to be proud of. But in the process of issuing our shares, we managed to educate the black community that there are things called "shares" and that they could start experiencing that free enterprise system by participating in the shareholding of, and getting dividends from, the company.

NSB's growing sales: The company has been growing in leaps and bounds. When we took over the company, the turnover was about 300 million rands; our turnover now is in excess of half a billion rands. The total capital we have employed is close to about 200 million rands. And all those resources, ladies and gentlemen, are managed by blacks, despite all this apartheid system and despite the whole skepticism that exists in the minds of many people that blacks cannot do anything positive.

We are predominantly involved in the sorghum beer industry. That's why we call the company National Sorghum Breweries. However, we have diversified within a short space of time. We have acquired one of the subsidiaries of Premier, Jabula Foods, so we're now involved in the food industry. The kind of products we sell are foods that are in demand in some of the squatter camps—vitamin-enriched products, protein- enriched products—and it's one of the areas we would like to expand.

We are involved in the soft drink business and we are also just in the process now of completing our first laager beer brewery, which is a multi-million rand project. People keep asking us, "How can you expect to compete with the giant South African Breweries?" Our intention is not necessarily to compete with anyone; our intention is to enable the black people who are actually consuming this product to have also a stake in the company that produces a particular product. National Sorghum Breweries is the first company that is enabling the people to have a hand in the production arena.

We have an excellent distribution system. We are scattered throughout the whole country, from Pietersberg right down to Cape Town. That's where our operations are actually located; therefore, we have the infrastructure to distribute any other products that we produce in the future.

Supporting black business: As part of the black economic empowerment exercise, our company sources most products and services from black business. For example, our printing and legal services are provided by black companies. And I can tell you now that they provide high quality products and services.

NSB, as part of its contribution to the black community, has a R30 million education trust, which sponsors blacks in fields of study to which black people were not exposed in the past: areas like agricultural science, engineering, finance and commerce. We are not funding people, for instance, who want to study philosophy. We are not saying it is not important, but we believe that we can better use of our money in the areas where there is a shortage of expertise among our people.

So, ladies and gentlemen, I want to say to you that if you are looking for prosperity in the new South Africa, if you are looking for the stability in the new South Africa, we need to involve the black community within the mainstream economy of the country rather than relegating it to the periphery. Thus, I am

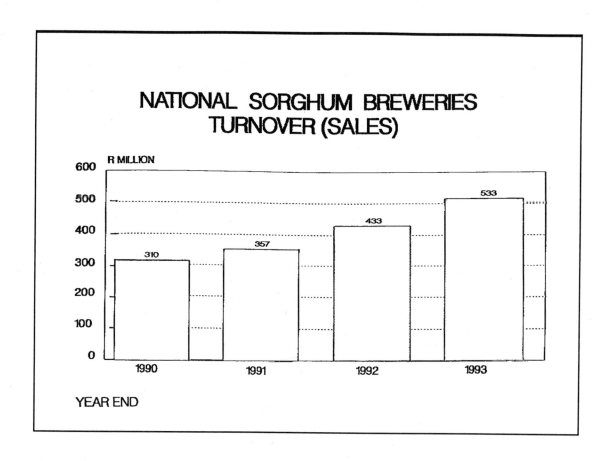

NATIONAL SORGHUM BREWERIES TURNOVER (SALES)

R MILLION

- 1990: 310
- 1991: 357
- 1992: 433
- 1993: 533

YEAR END

excited to hear what OPIC is saying about involving the black community. To those American companies that want to come into the country — and I want to mention that American companies are really known for their progressive recruitment and employment policies — we are urging you to continue with this approach and to please get involved with and support black businesses. Thank you very much.

ANNETTE HUTCHINS

The parent company of Soft Sheen International Foundation is Soft Sheen Products, an ethnic hair care company that does about $90 to $100 million worth of business here in the United States. About five years ago Soft Sheen Products started an expansion. It has a company in Kingston, Jamaica, where it manufactures in a joint venture relationship there. It purchased Dyke and Dryden, which is the largest minority-owned business in the U.K. It has moved into Brazil, where it manufactures under contract to Darrow Laboratories.

U.S. government services

Soft Sheen's investigation of the southern African market initially began in Zimbabwe. The organization that actually introduced Soft Sheen to South Africa, and introduced me to Soft Sheen, was the U.S. Department of Commerce. I was living in Harare, Zimbabwe, as director of the U.S.-Zimbabwe Business Council. I accompanied a delegation of black Zimbabweans on a visit to the Department of Commerce, where we met with Emily Solomon, who was then the desk officer for Zimbabwe and is now the desk officer for South Africa, with the under secretary for Africa from the Department of Commerce. Coca Cola was hosting President Robert Mugabe of the Republic of Zimbabwe. Soft Sheen Products happened to be one of the companies there at that meeting. The Department of Commerce often does these kinds of roundtable discussions.

The Council had just had *Essence Magazine*, which is the leading black female magazine, do a 15-page article on Zimbabwe, which Soft Sheen had read. They asked me if I would work for them in Chicago. I think it was January, February, and I told them, "No, I'm going back to Zimbabwe. It's too cold." But the staff person persisted. On the day of departure for Zimbabwe, I was asked to make a presentation to the management team. So I came en route to London for three hours in Chicago to make a presentation to them.

One of the things that I think is very important in the process of finding black partners is for the company to educate itself. Soft Sheen began the process of educating itself some two, three years ago now, because its management team was not familiar with Southern Africa. So Soft Sheen embarked upon a two-year educational process of the region, and that March or April I hosted them in Zimbabwe with assistance from U.S. Ambassador to Zimbabwe James Rawlings, who was formerly the president of Union Carbide's Africa region. Mr. Rawlings is a fantastic human being, extremely committed to the development of Africa

---

Annette Hutchins was formerly the Director of the Soft Sheen International Foundation.

in terms of business interests. He is now retired, but working still with Zimbabwe interests with Union Carbide. So we hosted them in Zimbabwe, but the presentation was on the region, including South Africa.

The Soft Sheen team visited three to four countries in Southern Africa. And to Emily's dismay, when we got to South Africa, we were taken around by the U.S. commercial attache, who now works for Soft Sheen in South Africa. So poaching is also one way, which we don't advise, of finding black partners. [Laughter] And I say that very seriously. Obviously, companies want to get up and go and move toward that profit goal, so that many companies do not want to invest a lot of time in training. Many companies are coming in and looking for people who are already in places and, fortunately or unfortunately, offering them large salaries to move from wherever they are now.

Now, the problem with that is that you're not investing in the development of person power in South Africa. Soft Sheen was created by three educators from the Chicago school system, so the philosophy of the company is very strongly committed to education. A theme of the foundation is education. It is a very entrepreneurial company and not really, I would say, a corporate structure. It believes in educating the consumer and the entrepreneur, and in providing or assisting that entrepreneur in identifying capital to start their own business.

Other organizations to consult

We also went, for instance, to visit IRRC where we met Meg [Voorhes] and the other staff of IRRC, and further educated the management team. I think that conferences like this are tremendous, but one of the problems is that it is always difficult to get the VP and the president to come to a conference and sit in the conference for one day. So we had to come up with other strategies, i.e., bring the VP down to the office for half an hour meeting with the staff of IRRC so that he could hear what some of the issues are, because I do believe that the commitment, particularly to move into areas that companies see as high risk, must be driven from the top.

Once in South Africa we began identifying institutions that were credible. Also in Washington we continued meetings with Sylvia Gon from the South Africa Foundation and with Lindiwe Mabuza of the African National Congress. We also met with the ANC in South Africa and with other political parties there. We met with a wide spectrum of organizations working on South Africa and got names from them of people working on South Africa.

Identifying potential black partners and staff

When we got to South Africa, we went to talk to those people whose names we had collected over the six months, to make a determination whether some of them would fit into our corporate culture as we moved ahead. Soft Sheen then felt, as it assessed and did a market study of the industry, that the industry standards needed to be upgraded. Because of apartheid, black South Africans were not able to go to some of the cosmetology schools and to take the trade test. Consequently, there are not very many black licensed cosmetologists in South Africa.

Having said that, the industry is present and very viable. However, since our products are on the upper end of the scale, we felt we needed to contribute to the upgrading of the industry with an education and training initiative. So we developed a foundation whose commitment is to education and training in the industry with a strong small business development component. From our experience in the United States and around the world, we believe many small businesses fail because they don't understand the cash flow cycle. So we not only train on product usage in cosmetology; we also have a very strong component on financial management and on how to set up and run a small business.

The other thing that we did was to ask our lawyers and our accounting firm to help us develop a process by which we could identify both staff and black board members to work with us.

We also commissioned three firms to help us identify people who would come and work for us. We had an experience with this in London where we had commissioned one firm, and the firm came back to us and said that they could not find any black people in the U.K. that could manage the operation or be our chief fiscal officer. So we went to London, talked to many black organizations and took to our search firm a list of 100 names of people we wanted them to vet for that purpose.

We did a similar thing in South Africa. For a year we followed *Enterprise* magazine, which is one of the South African magazines that focuses on black businesses and black business leaders. We got a copy of the *Portfolio of Black Business*. We went to the Small Business Development Corp. and talked to Mandy Maepa, the community relations officer there, and got a list of names from her. There are a number of black publications or publications that are geared toward the black market, like *Pace* magazine and *Tribute*, and we subscribed to those magazines to get names of people in the business areas where we were interested and we talked to those people about what we were doing.

Through the U.S. Department of Commerce, there is a visitors' program that is operated by the U.S. embassy to send South African groups to the United States. One group, Fabcos, was sponsored in this way and came to visit Soft Sheen, and we discovered that Fabcos has a cosmetology association along with 20 or 30 other associations in its grouping. We also discovered the Soweto Chamber of Commerce and various associations. And based on what we were interested in, we selected those organizations that we felt had something to offer us, or were interested in areas where we were interested. We went to talk with those people to begin the process of setting up our boards and our operation in South Africa.

I am pleased to report that we are scheduled to start our educational training center on Feb. 1, 1994, and we're in the process now of making our final decisions on staff and board members.

JOHN L. SIMS

I want to applaud and endorse what the previous speakers on this panel have said. As a result of their contributions, my own remarks have been considerably shortened, and I thank them for their contribution to my speech.

I want to talk, then, about Digital specifically. I spent most of my working life as an executive with Digital Equipment Corp. and had for 22 years wanted to do something in South Africa. I, fortunately, was part of our investment strategy in the Far East, in the Middle East, in South America. I had a financial and investment frame of the corporation. And I suddenly realized that I needed to prepare myself very differently for the question: Should Digital invest in South Africa?

So I set out to prepare myself, to sell the notion that South Africa and the region was viable for Digital, and Digital was not foreign to Africa. We had made investments in 13 other countries, but South Africa was very different. And those of you who are sitting here in this room contemplating the question "Should I invest?" should look at South Africa and feel the country. I did all of the things that Annette did and talked about in my own exploration as I prepared myself to sell this to our board of directors. I also spent two and a half years talking to everybody I could find in South Africa, everybody in Europe, almost every government agency in the United States. But, most importantly, I talked to the people in South Africa.

I talked to the black people in South Africa. I talked to every major business executive in South Africa, and I got a feeling about that country that was what I thought I would feel when I went with the question of should we invest in South Africa. It's a lovely place. The people are lovely, the weather there is marvelous, and it's a place that's going to grow and where you can have a business future. I concluded that I needed a three-tiered strategy if, in fact, I was going to have the ability to carry this message through our board.

Making business sense

First and foremost, the business piece had to be sound. That was easy, believe it or not. The only market, outside of some of the consumer goods that had shown growth over the 18 quarters of a descending economy was the informa-

John L. Sims is the president of the South Africa Free Election Fund and was formerly a vice president of Digital Equipment Corp.

tion technology market. In South Africa it was about $2 billion a year with a modest growth rate every year. That's the business that Digital is in. We talked to our worldwide customers, many of which had never left South Africa, who put us in a position that we could enter into that marketplace with a customer base such that, conceivably — and it's turning out to be the case — we could break even within a calendar year, a very persuasive argument. There is no issue worth following up on for an American business if it doesn't make business sense, and South Africa makes business sense.

Commitment to community

The second tier of the program that I presented talked about how, as good corporate citizens, the way we operate all over the world, we would have to have a major commitment to the communities in which we did business. We chose a program that has stood well for us here in the States, Project Reach, where we develop leaders in the black community for leadership in that community both at the entrepreneurial level and at the educational level. It's been terribly successful here; it's being adapted for South Africa.

Recruiting black staff and partners

The third is that we were going to have blacks as part of our business structure. We were first going to have black employees become part of the management structure to set the tone for this question. Our two top people in South Africa are a white male from Geneva and a black woman from the United States. We had to wrestle with the issue: Can we find the kind of talent we need to initially populate our office? We were very fortunate. There are a lot of black South African trained technologists both in South Africa and sitting outside of South Africa. But the talent is there. It's old talent; it needs to be retrained, but that's possible. Our business is growing in a very balanced way; we have as many black technical people in South Africa working for Digital as we do white South Africans.

The other piece of our commitment to having blacks participate in our business was identifying black businesses. We made up our mind before we went into South Africa we were prepared to do one of three things: Our first choice, of course, was to find a black business that needed nothing from us other than an opportunity to be our business partner. The second, which we were prepared to do if we had to, was to find some talented people and develop them into a business, where we would carry the responsibility of the development for up to two years. And the third option was to bring black talent into the company, develop it specific to our business, and then spin it off.

What we were able to find in South Africa, at least today, is a business that we've labeled a value-added re-seller. A value-added re-seller in the high tech industry is a specialist in a given segment of the market. They take our product, add their products or technology to it and sell it to the banking industry, the beer industry, the mining industry. We give them technology product at a favorable price and support their banking relationships. We have such a partner in South Africa. It's a struggle, but it is an issue that is solvable. It is going, and I think it's only going to go very well.

I would strongly advise you to think about South Africa as a business, to think about the mission that David [Cralle] talks about, to think about all the issues that have been raised here. The market is viable, the region is the gateway of all of Africa. By the year 2010 that region will be in the top five in the world as an economic development area. There are going to be billions of dollars made. That's why I fundamentally believe that the country is going to stabilize, it's going to have a free election, and it's going to be a place where one can do the kind of work that we've learned to do in the United States, where fairness and equality is not separate from the business and profit that will grow a strong and positive economy.

LIONEL GREWAN

My topic this afternoon is a relatively simple one in that I need to share with you some of the work that my organization does down in the Natal area. Before I get into my text, let me just preface this by saying the approach that we have to the work I'm going to describe is very much a bottoms-up one, which leaves me with a foot in two camps: one within the corporate environment, and the other one within the small business sector. Second, the work that I am about to describe to you is certainly the beginning of a process, and then, third, that this work is a voluntary approach and it comes at the behest of a number of the companies.

Black business success stories

If past performance is a useful measure of the potential to survive and thrive in the future, then I would like you to consider the following: Jabu Madlala launched an organization called JBN Technology Services in 1990. He offers computer training to students and corporate employees. Currently, his little organization has 12 full-time employees, and his business turns over in excess of R500,000 per annum.

Sipho Makhanya runs an organization called Sunset Clothing. He sells uniforms and protective clothing. His small business brings in about 240,000 rand annually. Moses Malo is the chairman of X.B. Brokers, which is a financial services business. This three-year-old company looks after 7 billion rands' worth of insurance and burial society business.

Mrs. Nomadlobi Vukama is a prominent businesswoman who runs a BP petrol service station in Guguletu in the Cape Town township.

Moses Mcinga is the managing director of Black Moses Distribution Company. Moses distributes products in township areas. After six years of operation, the company owns 35 vehicles ranging from light delivery vans to big rigs and turns over in excess of 20 million rand per annum.

Mohale Mohanyele, who happens to be the chairman of National Sorghum Breweries, runs the largest black-owned business in South Africa. And National Sorghum Breweries currently turns over in excess of 600 million rand per annum.

What I'm sharing with you is a very small sample of successful businesses that are set to grow in the future, and what is significant is that in spite of the past

---

Lionel Grewan is the executive director of the National Economic Initiative, in South Africa.

inhibiting legislation in South Africa, black business has made progress against all odds. With the demise of apartheid, it will not be long before black Oppenheimers emerge.

The National Economic Initiative

I want to tell you a little bit about the National Economic Initiative, the organization that I represent. Let me give you a brief background as to how the organization got started. By 1989 a number of American companies that originally were present in the Natal area had disinvested from South Africa. In the Natal area, where there had been 12 American companies, by 1989 there were only four: Mobil Oil, Masonite, Otis Elevators, and Richards Bay Minerals. Those four companies wanted to continue some of the work that they had begun within the Sullivan Program and to look for a way to develop this in the Natal area. I was invited to see if I could get that started, which I did.

By 1990, these four U.S. subsidiary companies got together to launch the organization, whose mission is to develop the economy through black/white economic partnerships. The main focus of the organization is to identify business opportunities in the large companies and then find small firms that could be matched with these opportunities. The NEI currently has a membership of some 80 corporations and an equal number of small business members who are primarily black. The organization is two and a half years old.

In facilitating this matchmaking role, the NEI has a very structured program. The first step in the process is to identify small businesses that have been in operation for at least two years. This target group has survived the initial start-up phase, and in all cases the necessary technical skills are present.

Each of the small businesses identified are graded in order to assess their capabilities. Some 450 small businesses were identified and were entered into an electronic database. Corporate members have access to the database, which is updated regularly. Increasing the number of entries in the database and adding new names to the list is an ongoing process. Corporate members are made aware of the directory, which is mailed to them. Each corporate member is targeted and the commitment of the chief executive officer to encourage the use of small businesses is initially sought.

Most CEOs appear to support this out-contracting initiative; however, further meetings with the buying or purchasing departments are necessary to allay their fears of incompetence on the part of small business. It is then necessary to build the relationship between the small and the corporate business, as both have operated in separate environments and some common ground has to be found. This is done through the promotion of visits by the small business to corporate premises, and during these corporate business opportunity visits, the small business representative is taken on a tour of the factory premises and business opportunities are identified. The tour ends with discussion of the opportunities that were identified, and a relationship begins from that point onwards. Once a contract has been signed, support is provided to the small business. This support can take the form of providing business or technical skills training, and the NEI arranges for this to take place.

To facilitate this matchmaking process, a project was recently embarked upon to establish what we call a business opportunity center, and this was launched in March of 1993. The center provides the conduit for corporations to channel business opportunities to small businesses. Corporations requiring the service of small business can send their request to the center. Small business operators visit the center regularly to see what corporate requirements are and then to respond to them. Services are the main request, but some items for manufactures are also requested.

The manufacturing sector of small business is growing much slower than the services sector. This is largely because of the difficulty in obtaining finance from the financial institutions. In summary, the NEI program is making good progress, and in the first six months of 1993, more than R600,000 changed hands. That's the good news. The bad news is, if we were able to get each of those 80 corporations to take a more aggressive position in developing smaller businesses, then the target that we set up of turning over a million rand a month between these two sectors is really achievable, so from that perspective the larger companies do need a whole lot of prodding. Although there is this commitment at corporate level, we still need to get them actually to put into practice some of these commitments that they have in principle.

Other initiatives to develop black business

The NEI program is only one attempt at developing black suppliers. Others committed to developing suppliers include Anglo-American, Gencor, Johannesburg Consolidated Investments and Anglo-Vaal. These mining houses have recognized the need to develop black suppliers and have active programs. One program that needs special mention is Anglo-American Corporation's small business unit, Lytet. This unit was established four years ago with the objective of developing black businesses by taking equity in the firms and providing the necessary management skills to ensure success. Financial loans at prime rates are offered to the small business. Currently 10 companies have been established, and they have a collective annual turnover in excess of R25 million. Masakhane Cleaning Services cleans hostels and offices and has an annual turnover of some R4 million. Simunye is a drag line cleaning and bucket refurbishment business that operates on Anglo's coal mines; 1992 saw Simunye turn over in excess of R3 million. These are just two examples of business opportunities that were identified, and through corporate involvement have become success stories.

At the Nafcoc Annual Convention that was held in July of 1993, Archie Nkonyeni, the president of Nafcoc, stated that apartheid was over, and there can be no more excuses for the lack of initiative on the part of both black and whites. Political power without full economic participation will not be meaningful. As South Africa moves toward democracy and international acceptability, the U.S. companies are reviewing their investment policies towards our country. We welcome their return to South Africa but will request that they do business differently. In a nutshell, it is not business as usual.

We want to see joint venture companies between black and U.S. corporations being established, and in this particular regard, I would like to pay tribute to Digital and Thebe Investments, who have set the trend for other corporations to follow. Black businesses are developing at a rapid rate and have taken a positive view of the future. The recent creation of the Women's Development Bank, and the joint venture between the giant insurance group, Metropolitan Life, and a group of black businessmen to create an organization called Methold is further evidence of the dynamic new trends that are being set.

The U.S., through support for sanctions, played a major role in bringing about change in South Africa. Now the U.S. is once again poised to play a major role in South Africa, this time through constructive engagement and development.

I would like to thank Meg and the IRRC for having provided this opportunity for me to share some of the work that we do in South Africa with South African companies and with smaller black owned companies. I think the importance of what I'm saying to you today has been realized within my country. And, with U.S. companies coming in, this black business development activity can only be accelerated.

GEORGE F. LINDEQUE

Good afternoon, ladies and gentlemen. My name is George Lindeque, and I work for a company called Escom. Today has been a very emotional experience for me, because the first time I came to the United States, about 30 years ago, I was the personal assistant and private secretary to, in your terminology, South Africa's secretary of state. The purpose of that visit was to state the case for apartheid at the United Nations and then here in Washington with the American government. So, in fact, the first time around I came to the United States to defend apartheid. Today I'm here to try to explain to you how things have changed, and also to deal with my own transformation over a period of 30 years. Hence, it is emotional for me to be here today.

My company has long been perceived as part of the problem because we are a parastatal, and we are linked to the government. The perception about Escom is that we supported the government in what it did. I'd like to indicate to you that my company, in fact, is part of the solution, and that we have initiated many initiatives to effect change, not only in my company but also in South Africa. Your stance on apartheid has sped up this process of change. We are now in the phase of catch-up; we are now in the phase of redressing and improving, and today for me personally has been a very important learning experience.

The challenges facing Escom

Because we are a large company, we play a significant role in South Africa, and we have four main challenges that we have to deal with. Our first challenge is to deal with the political realities that are emerging in South Africa now. We are dealing with the expectations of our employees; we are dealing with resistance to change by our employees; we are dealing with polarization, and conflict, and rejection, and we are dealing with anger on both sides of the race spectrum. And that puts us right in the political arena.

We also have to deal with some of the economic realities of South Africa, which you've heard about, and we believe that we have an important key role to play to generate economic growth in South Africa. We are dealing as a company with equalizing opportunities in creating access and dealing with the world of work, which is different from what we were used to.

George F. Lindeque is the executive director for human resources at Escom, South Africa's national electric utility.

The third challenge we are dealing with as a company is our involvement in education, housing and electrification. The fact of the matter is that the education system has not delivered the black workers we require to manage a highly sophisticated, capital-intensive industry. And last, the fourth challenge is the challenge of being a role model, the challenge of using our power and influence to play a lead role in reconciling the issues that we have to deal with as a business and in assisting reconstruction.

I'd like to give you some basic facts about my company, so to put these things in perspective. I'd like to tell you something very briefly about the electrification program. Then I would like to deal with an initiative or strategy that we launched in Escom called harmonization, to be in harmony with the environment that's changing around us. And then I'd like to conclude with why we are doing these things.

Escom was established in 1922. Our governance structure is on a two-tier basis: The government appoints our policymaking body, which is called the Electricity Council, and the Council appoints the executive. I'm part of that executive. We employ 42-odd-thousand people; 70 percent of whom belong to 10 different unions. We generate 90 percent of the power in South Africa, which equates to 60 percent of the power generated in Africa. We are the fourth largest electricity utility internationally, measured against capacity and sales. The geographic reach of the power network we operate is equivalent to the combined area of France, Germany and Italy.

Like many South African companies, despite the fact that 50 percent of the employees are white and the other 50 percent are black, 90 percent of our managers are still white males. The reality we face is that 20 percent of our employees, black employees essentially, are functionally illiterate. But I think the most disconcerting thing about Escom and about South Africa is that 60 percent of the population of South Africa do not have access to our product.

Escom's business strategies

Since 1985, we initiated major change strategies in the company, for a variety of reasons, which eventually culminated or were distilled into four major business strategies, the first one being: Business efficiency is key to our survival. We have to be strong economically and financially to be able to deal with the changes confronting us in South Africa. And that puts us into the economic development business of the country.

A second strategy in Escom, which occupies our minds every day, is the issue of electrification, which I'll come back to. The third is harmonization. These two together put us in a quality of life and social reconstruction business, which makes us an important player in the South African economy.

And then the fourth one is a very simple one, and that is making it happen, because we believe it's no good talking about these things; we have to actively lead, and lead the country in where we want and have to go.

A few things about electrification: In 1987 we said, "Electricity for all," and it took us four years to get going. There are 25 million people who don't have access to electricity, which translates into about four to five million households. Last year we succeeded in making 200,000 new connections, which translates into a million people. There are more than 450 distributors of electricity with 2,000 different retail tariff prices throughout the country. The industry has to be restructured and rationalized if we are going to be serious about electricity for all. And the reality is, electricity has become politicized in South Africa, from the white side and from the black side; it's a tough situation.

At this stage, we have to manage a bad debt in excess of R600 million because of the politicization of electricity. We have to, we believe, as a country and with the other distributors, effect more than 500,000 connections per annum at the cost of R1.2 billion. The whole project in the next four to five years will be in excess of R12 billion. It's a massive challenge, and it's a massive challenge also in terms of training.

But beyond electrification in South Africa, we believe there is a bigger role for Escom in the broad economic development of the region, because many of the problems of the region can, in fact, be resolved through electrification. In the sub-Saharan region more than 200 million people don't have access to electricity, another massive challenge that we are going for.

The need for 'social harmonization'

I'd like to talk about social harmonization. In your terminology, perhaps the term would be employment equity and affirmative action, as we heard discussed this morning. In 1980 I was co-author of the following statement: "Escom has long realized the necessity to eliminate this racial discrimination and to change the labor pattern. Escom is endeavoring to create better work opportunities for all population groups in our employ within the framework of existing legislation." This was a paradox, because there in the last phrase we neutralized ourselves. But for that time a very bold statement, very bold indeed.

In 1985 we realized we were not doing that well at all. We became bolder. We identified 150-odd discriminatory practices in Escom —the overt stuff, the things that you could see and with the stroke of a pen, we established parity in terms of conditions of service with regard to gender and race for more than 13,000 employees, and we back-dated it for two years.

And then we started getting involved in education. This year we will probably be investing more than R20 million, which will impact more than 600,000 black school children in respect of teacher development, scholarships at schools, electrification of schools, and the establishment of resource centers right from pre-primary through to secondary schools — a massive initiative on our side, we believe. It's part of trying to redress the institutional fabric that Bob Tucker spoke about earlier on.

Our scholarship program is also fairly extensive. At any point in time we support about 1500 students through scholarships at the various tertiary institutions in South Africa. Our policy is that every year we have to grant 25 percent of the new scholarships to people of color. This has changed the profile of our scholarships; now 30 percent of our scholarships are people of color, which we are very proud of.

In the company we also have accelerated black development programs through mentorship in a variety of regions, a big pool of people that we are preparing for the future. The impact of this is that our profile is slowly but surely changing. At the top of the house, where we are 20 people, five are now people of color. It wasn't like that one year ago, and we still want to change it even further. Our big problem, though, is at the bottom end of the house. Every year we invest more than R300 million in training and development, professionally and otherwise, using facilities at book value to the extent of R450 million, which is a business in excess of, say, R750 million But the problem is that the right people aren't getting the money. We are still sitting with the functionally illiterate, and we have to shift that, and we've set ourselves a goal that we will change that within the next few years.

We are also now involved in black businesses; two years ago we weren't. This year we estimate we will spend more than R5 million for the establishment of black business people to supply us with things that we need.

Lastly, on harmonization, we started an initiative a year ago which we called "creating a process whereby employees can meaningfully influence the decision-making process and strategic direction of Escom." The net effect of that is we now have three trade unionists on our governing council. In practical terms, that means the people that I negotiated "contracts" with, in your terminology, are now my bosses. Two of the new council members represent civic associations. It has an immense impact on the strategic direction of Escom. We also have a consultive forum of our black employees, and I'm proud to say I'm their patron, where we are creating processes whereby they can meaningfully influence the strategic direction of Escom.

Why Escom is changing

Why are we doing all of these apparently nice things? I think first of all we're doing it because it's the right thing to do, and we should have started a long time ago, and now we have to go into top gear. Second, we believe that it's important to do these things because that's how we're going to attain the long-term business viability and business growth of Escom. Third, we're doing it because

Escom is an integral part of the emerging nonracial, democratic South Africa. Fourth, we're doing it because we are in the economic development, and quality of life, and social reconstruction business. We have no choice; we have to do it. Our customer base is changing rapidly.

We are doing it fifthly because we still have a long way to go to achieve equality and equity. We are in catch-up mode now. We are doing it because we want to develop an organization where race and gender are not issues, and where only ability and performance are the key things. We are doing it because we are a strong company, and we think we can take leadership, and we think we can lead the corporate world into a situation which they don't know. We are doing it because we believe the mind-set of South African business has to be changed for economic and social revival, and that black people have to be developed.

And lastly, ladies and gentlemen, we are doing it because we believe in the potential of South Africa and the sub-continent; we believe in the well-being of our country and of our people; and we believe in the prosperity, and therefore the prosperity scenario presented this morning appeals to me. We have to do it; otherwise, we're going to go down the tubes. Remember, Africa has fallen off the map. We've got to put Africa back on the map in terms of the globalization that's happening now.

I'd like to say thank you to Meg Voorhes for arranging this. It's an honor for me to stand here—I really mean that.

WYNAND PRETORIUS

First, before I start addressing the theme of our panel, "Developing Black Suppliers and Managers," let me address two issues that were raised this morning, because I'm sure many of you have questions about how to approach the emerging new South Africa, and perhaps—for those of you who are already operating business there—how to expand your businesses.

Two issues: the statement that conditionality for investors is unacceptable; and also the perceived need that the future government must intervene. I think we must be realistic; what we need is a balanced approach. There is broad-based consensus in our country that we should use all our macro policies to achieve certain economic and social goals. Past intervention created many distortions and in order to facilitate the process to transform South African society, intervention by a future government is axiomatic. In a democratic order where all processes are transparent, intervention and conditionality are useful policy instruments.

The whole question of institutional reform is quite an interesting debate. You know, I joined one of the biggest Broederbond institutions in the country in the 1970s—I was very young—and I thought that by using the correct strategies, it would be possible to reform an institution like that from within. But it was not even a year before I realized that it was impossible to reform apartheid.

And in 1980, my research unit at Rand Afrikaans University started building linkages, strategizing and forming alliances with community groups outside the university, and I think today we have one of the best track records in respect of functional literacy training programs for adults in transport operations management and also in capacity building in general among community groups such as the trade unions, the local civic associations, the transportation desk of the ANC and Nafcoc, the black business chamber.

And really, for those of you who have been close to South Africa, if you want to assist in the development of black suppliers and managers, my advice to you is to become involved with the 3-4-5-6 empowerment program of Nafcoc, and I'm sure Professor Sethi will touch on that.

Now, a little bit of information about the transport industry. First, transport is viewed in the country by the government-in-waiting as an essential service, but

---

Wynand Pretorius heads the Department of Transport Economics at Rand Afrikaans University.

there is very little support for this view, unfortunately, with the current regime. The reason why transport is an essential service: the majority of our people are dependent on public passenger transport. On any given day, 85 percent of our people are dependent on public passenger transport to get to and from places of work. If you take motor vehicle ownership, among white households, there are approximately 420 vehicles per 500 household, compared with fewer than 60 among 500 black households.

Apartheid's legacy in the transport sector

One of the legacies of apartheid, and a very serious structural distortion that will be with us for a long time, concerns commuting distances. You are talking, in the case of the minibus industry approximately 20 kilometers, for the train passengers 30 kilometers, and for bus passengers in excess of 40 kilometers one way. In the African context, you are talking very long distances. More important, the average trip of 40 kilometers combined with walking may take two to three hours both in the morning and again in the evening. Some passengers are traveling in excess of 100 kilometers one way. Thus, approximately 30 percent of private consumption expenditure goes toward transport. Now those are the kind of distortions that will be with us for a long time.

And you cannot rely on market forces only to resolve those kind of issues. We will have to intervene over the short and medium term. So it is against that background that we need to set conditions, to develop codes, that are capable of really empowering the disenfranchised citizens of our population who constitute the majority of people.

If you look at the role that transport can play in the actual transformation of our country, and specifically in the rural context, some 25 percent of our rural children aged 7 to 10 don't go to school for the simple reason that the schools are not accessible. The distances to and from the schools are too far for children in that age bracket. Against this background, we need a government that is concerned about the real needs on the ground and prepared to do something to correct the social distortions. If you take the infant mortality rate, and compare that to the urban areas, in the rural areas you are talking about 100 deaths per thousands, whereas in the urban areas it is less than 10.

It is against that background that it is most important for us to create policy frameworks as well as programs that are capable of addressing the distortions on the ground. And I think that there is broad-based consensus that this is the way for us to go.

Developing black transport managers and suppliers

I was asked also to share with you what can actually be done to develop black suppliers and managers. Again here, some statistics. We started with our functional literacy training programs in 1980. If you do a sectoral analysis of the transport sector, say, compared to manufacturing, which is currently the single largest contributor to our gross domestic product, the number of black people employed in the middle and senior management of the transport sector is approximately 35 percent, compared to manufacturing, where it is 15 percent, and to mining, where it is less than 10 percent. From 1980 until now, my unit's programs alone have already trained more than 17,000 students; they're employed by parastatals, government organizations, the private sector, research institutions. In fact, we have assisted the first black transport economists to set themselves up as a consultancy. So there is a lot that can be done. The programs are there.

What we need is support, because we have a government that is disinvesting from tertiary education in real terms. The universities are struggling. We have a subsidy formula where if we need $100, the government will only give us $60. The cutback is very significant, and since more than 90 percent of the university's expenditure is operating costs, we are not talking about capital programs that one can manage and manipulate over a period of time. So we are forced to cut back on our support programs. This is an area where we, perhaps in concert with international supporters, can put pressure on the interim government.

Another characteristic of our programs: We link them to business opportunities for disenfranchised people. We have started a program in response to requests from our constituencies—trade unions, Nafcoc, the ANC transport desk—to identify opportunities in the transport sector. I want to share with you the following ideas.

A significant number of firms in South Africa operate transport divisions, but don't view these divisions as essential to their companies. Therefore, we approach these companies and ask them if they would be willing to disinvest in transport and to make their transport functions available to the people who are currently operating that service. The majority of truck drivers in South Africa are black. On average, a very significant number of the people involved in the transport function are black.

Based on the win-win principles, we can assure the firm that in terms of cost and quality, they will not be worse off, if they disinvest in transport. We have a funny phenomenon that firms are increasing their asset base all the time because they don't know what to do with their excess surplus capital. That is why firms are investing in transport even though it is not their core business. We convince them there is nothing to lose in cost or quality if they turn those operations over to their staff.

Now, just some practical problems on the ground: the financial institutions, it was mentioned by Bob [Tucker], control a very significant amount of money but only a very small portion of that is currently in use by black entrepreneurs. The problem is that the banks are honestly not in a position, in my opinion, to assess the relative risk factor associated with a black enterprise. You have the situation where perhaps a fairly young white male at the bank will talk to a black person. There is a language problem. There is not enough information about what is going on in the townships. There is not enough information as to the exact profiles and competence levels within the black sector of our population.

On average, a black person is viewed as a higher risk and businesses managed by black people are viewed as high risk businesses. If any white person approached a bank in South Africa to ask for vehicle finance, he will get the finance at least 5 percent cheaper than the average black person. And it should exactly be the other way around, if banks are to help transform the base of the economy. Therefore, part of our program is to make finance available to black entrepreneurs. We have established a vehicle finance foundation for this purpose.

Another problem area is insurance. The cost of vehicle insurance, public liability and goods in transit, etc., to a black person is very, very high. That is an area we need to address. For those of you who are currently involved in those services and products, this is an opportunity for you in South Africa.

Lastly, on the whole question of business support, there are many, many systems available. In the United States, the majority of commercial vehicles are in the hands of owner-drivers. There are tremendous support programs for them, operated through such organizations as the American Trucking Association, which is an association of associations, and what we are trying to do is to access those support programs so that it is not necessary for us to reinvent the wheel. What I think is very important is for people in the international community to make bursaries available so that we can develop more and more black transport economists and people who are capable of managing transport undertakings. Just to give you an idea of the need out there, in any given year, 200 students are registered for formal training in the transport sector with our institution alone.

Outlook

I want to conclude with a certain perspective. I know that you have many questions about South Africa, but the region has lots of opportunities. What I would like to share with you is that the preferential trade area, which is most of the [African] countries south of the equator, are reviewing all of their investment codes and business practices, and the overall objective is to try to standardize these policy documents and frameworks in general. If we look at the potential of the region as a whole, we are talking about a market, depending on how you define it, with a population of 120 to 200 million people. The good news is that South Africa will become a signatory to the preferential trading agreement, and the signing ceremony is scheduled for November 1993.

We have got the resources and what I think is so wonderful, we have also got the leaders. Think of a person like Dr. Mandela. Even at a relatively conservative university such as mine, the Rand Afrikaans University, whenever he comes onto the campus, the students don't only want to see him, they want to touch him. We have leaders with vision, we have the scarce resources, we have a willing and able work force. What we need are friends like yourselves to support us in the process of transformation. The best option, when it comes to prediction and speculation about the future, is to make the future happen.

S. PRAKASH SETHI

Dear chairperson, honored guests, ladies and gentleman.

It is indeed a pleasure to be with you this afternoon. The focus of my remarks today is on black economic empowerment in South Africa. In particular, I would briefly reflect on two aspects of this problem. One, what is the future direction of economic and social conditions of the black majority of South Africa's citizens if current trends persist. I believe this situation to be quite distressing and unlikely to change unless a set of proactive and affirmative policies are adopted by the new government and the business community in the formal sector of South Africa. Therefore, I would like to outline an action plan that the new government and the business community in South Africa should pursue, and the black business community must demand, if there is to be any hope of measurable improvement in the economic situation of the vast majority of South Africa's people.

The optimists will tell us that a positive sea change has taken place in the political destiny of South Africa whose direction is clear and whose course is irreversible. Mr. Mandela and the ANC have called for the lifting of sanctions against investments in South Africa. They are urging the international investment community and lending institutions to return to South Africa and help in its economic development. This is an encouraging scenario.

Unfortunately, neither a political franchise nor democratic values can survive for any sustained period unless a majority of a nation's people share in its economic wealth, and where both opportunities for productive work and distribution of economic rewards are considered fair and equitable. To put it bluntly, political justice rings hollow unless accompanied by economic justice. This brings me to the second trend, and the one that I find most discouraging. It has to do with the dismal progress, or to be more exact, non-progress, that has occurred in the economic arena for the black people. Black economic empowerment has not moved much beyond slogans. None of the major indicators of black economic empowerment show any improvement. These include: the proportion of South African gross domestic product (GDP) produced by black-owned businesses; the proportion of national wealth and income-producing assets owned by blacks; the decline in unemployment rates; and the upward mobility of blacks in higher-paying jobs.

S. Prakash Sethi is the associate director of the Center for Management at Baruch College, The City University of New York.

What is even more disheartening is the fact that the new political leadership of South Africa does not appear to have given the problem the kind of attention that it seriously and urgently deserves. In his call to lift sanctions, Mr. Mandela at the United Nations did emphasize the need for channelling investments toward the black business community. However, there does not seem to be any systematic effort within the ANC's economic policy structure as to how the interests of black business community could be integrated into the formal sector of the economy.

One can also not depend on the normal market forces and the new political realities to persuade the formal business establishment in South Africa to create a significant and discernible shift in their business operations to accommodate black economic aspirations. Their record of accomplishments over the last 30 years, and even over the last five years, does not give one much optimism. Moreover, the recent statement by the South African Chamber of Business (SACOB) on affirmative action sounds more like "business as usual," rather than a recognition of the new reality and a need for taking more direct and forceful action. Relying on the usual escape hatch of calling everything that seeks accountability as "quotas," it wants the formal business sector of South Africa to be left alone to make the best faith effort without burdening them with any responsibility for showing what indeed is the best faith effort.

Let me emphasize that from my perspective the issue is not merely rhetorical or ideological. Instead, it is based on two sets of hard realities.

1. For the foreseeable future, most jobs and income for South Africa's black people will have to be created in the formal sector, and entrepreneurial opportunities in the small business sector. Without jobs, there could be no income, no increased consumer spending and no economic growth. In the absence of job-driven economic growth, there would be greater call for creating systems of welfare and income transfers from the productive to non-productive sectors that would further retard economic growth.

2. The current discrepancy in income, job opportunities and wealth accumulation, simply will not be tolerated in a society unless there is real evidence of concrete steps being taken to ameliorate these conditions. Left alone, the market simply will take too much time to correct, if ever, those inequalities because of the inherent deficiencies in the resource base and skill level of the two groups. *Therefore, there must be a judicious and restrained intervention in the market place* to channel more resources toward black economic growth both because it is economically rational and because it is morally right.

The goal of black economic empowerment

Black economic empowerment is not an end in itself, but a means to an end. The ultimate goal of black economic empowerment is to achieve economic parity among all groups in South Africa in proportion to their representation in the population. Since blacks in South Africa represent almost 75 percent of the total population, eventually they must also account for 75 percent of the nation's wealth and disposable income. The success of black economic empowerment strategies, therefore, must be measured in terms of the extent to which we move toward accomplishing the goal of economic parity.

We readily accept the notion that when it comes to individuals and not groups, income and wealth would, and should, differ considerably based on each individual's capacities and circumstances. I also realize that some differences in income, wealth and employment opportunities will persist for a long period of transition while underlying structural deficiencies are being corrected. Nor is it likely that we would ever achieve a perfect world. However, the test of our determination, and the success of our effort, must be evidenced through an accelerated and growing pace of narrowing inequalities of opportunities in the marketplace and a resultant narrowing of the gap in the national share of income, wealth, and control of productive assets among various groups.

Current economic status of blacks in South Africa

Optimists would tell you that blacks have made good progress in the economic arena. Many measures of apartheid have been relaxed or abandoned. And further reforms are on the horizon. For example, monthly household income of black households has risen over six times during the last 10 years to where it now stands at over R700.00. In the area of personal income, in 1985, whites accounted for 55.5 percent of personal disposable income while blacks accounted for 31.8 percent. According to University of South Africa estimates, by the year 2000, whites' share of disposable income is expected to decline to 42.5 percent while that of blacks to increase to 40.7 percent. This latter figure would represent a jump of 31 percent. Blacks currently account for over 40 percent of all retail purchases, a figure that is likely to increase to 50 percent or higher by the year 2000. Black wage rates are rising much faster than for white workers.

These numbers are interesting but we would be fooling ourselves if we regarded them as signs of progress. They do not even begin to address the serious deficiencies that exist. An overwhelming majority of blacks earn wages and live under conditions that are barely above the poverty level. This leaves them with little discretionary income for saving or investment in human capital, i.e., education and skills development. Unemployment rates among blacks average over 16 percent while those among black youths could be as high as 50 percent. These are the highest rates among all groups and affect those who can least afford it.

Moreover, regardless of all the progress made by the blacks in small business, this effort alone will not be enough to pull them out of poverty or enable them to compete with white business, not anytime soon, not in the foreseeable future, and perhaps never.

With few exceptions, black businesses concentrate primarily on serving the black community. They are engaged in low level service activity with a very small value added component. Most of them are one person owner-operated businesses designed to provide a meager source of income to the worker-owner who has been unable to find other employment. Even then, only about 2 percent of the black population is estimated to be involved in entrepreneurial activity as opposed to 12 percent of whites. The informal sector and small business are highly desirable, but they are not a panacea. Estimates show that black business accounts for less than 1 percent of the nation's GDP, and it sill would not amount to much even if it were to increase to 2 or 3 percent.

Nor are blacks doing well in the area of professional and managerial level employment in the formal economic sector. The number of black managers and administrators represents *less than 4 percent* of all persons in the supervisory category. Blacks are grossly under represented in the managerial and professional ranks even given the very low percentage rate of blacks graduating from professional and technical institutions. Current estimates suggest that there less than 250,000 blacks employed in the professional, administrative, and technical capacities where they occupy mostly the lower ranks of occupational ladders. The ANC has recently pointed to South Africa's dismaying racial and gender employment disparities, targeting these groups for affirmative-action programs. To wit, in the largest 100 South African companies, 97.5 percent of managers are white, while 92.5 percent are men. Furthermore, according to a recent study by the International Monetary Fund, a large part of the increase in the income share of the black work force in south Africa has come about through a narrowing of wage differential between whites and non-whites in similar job categories and not by increasing the number of blacks in higher-paying, more skilled, categories. Therefore, the fastest way to increasing black incomes is through better training and employment in higher skill jobs.

We should also accept it as a matter of reality that black prosperity in south Africa—at least during the next 20-25 years—will come largely from wages and salaries and not through income from capital and investments. Blacks currently own a little over 1 percent of this nation's wealth. Even a four-fold increase in those assets would not make a measurable dent in the black overall share of national income. Therefore, skill improvement must be our top priority. It would increase black penetration of management levels in the corporate sector. It would also improve the competitive strength of black-owned businesses by providing them with skilled professional and managerial people.

The representation of blacks in the corridors of corporate economic power is also abysmally low and prevents them from influencing major policy decisions. A preliminary analysis of data of the top 100 companies listed on the Johannesburg Stock Exchange (JSE) shows that of the approximately 2,550 total directorships available only about 30, or less than 2 percent, are occupied by black directors. The number of actual black directors is even lower because many of them hold multiple directorships. Regarding the issue of control of productive, or income producing assets in South Africa, one can count the number of black-owned or -controlled companies listed on the JSE on one hand.

It does no good to suggest that not enough skilled blacks are available to fill the upper ranks of corporate managers and professionals; that basic systems of education must be improved; and, that it takes time for people to gain training and experience to reach the upper echelons of management. Nor does it make much sense to offer black employees shares in large, publicly traded, companies. These shares may give them a feeling of well-being and ownership, but in practical terms their usefulness is extremely limited because the combined ownership of shares in all companies by blacks is not going to be high enough for them to have any influence on the South African business community; and the black share of ownership in individual companies would be so small as to preclude any possibility of their having a voice in the top management decision-making.

This line of reasoning, however, begs the question rather than answers it. If after all these years, the best the South African companies have been able to show is a measly 30 black directorships and 4 percent of managerial jobs, how long must we wait to see any evidence of further growth, especially when these companies refuse to offer specific plans and growth targets and reject all outside suggestions by labelling them "quotas" and therefore undesirable and unacceptable?

A new approach to black economic empowerment

It is apparent that structural changes must be made in South Africa's formal business sector. This would mean a system that is less concentrated and more competitive. This would mean a system that is open and accessible, and where top decision-makers reflect the broad characteristics of South African society rather than the narrow interests of the entrenched minority.

One such approach has been developed by Nafcoc [the National African Federated Chamber of Commerce] in 1990, which I helped develop. It is called the 3-4-5-6 plan. Its aim is to gain a fair share of the economic pie on the part of the black people of South Africa in terms of:

(a) integration of blacks into the formal sector through board memberships, increased jobs and upward mobility in the managerial ranks; and,

(b) expansion of entrepreneurship, and ownership of productive assets, by blacks in the formal sector.

The plan established a 10-year goal in various areas of corporate economic activity along the following lines:

- All companies listed on the JSE must have at least 30 percent of their board members from the black community;

- At least 40 percent of their shareholdings must be controlled by the black community;

- At least 50 percent of the value of their outside purchases must come from black-owned suppliers and contractors; and,

- At least 60 percent of their management ranks must be filled by members of the black community.

Since then the 3-4-5-6 plan has received widespread publicity and a large measure of hostility. The South African business community perceived it as a threat to its autonomy. It was also criticized for being too ambitious and impractical. We believe that a careful analysis of the plan would show it to be practicable and reasonable in its goals and expectations. I might also suggest that while these targets are established with primarily the South African companies in mind, they should be equally adaptable, with minor modifications, by foreign companies operating in South Africa.

Time does not permit me to make a detailed explanation of how this plan might be implemented. I would be happy to make this information available upon request. Let me, however, provide you with a brief description of how some of the plan elements would operate.

Representation on corporate boards: Let us look at the Nafcoc target calling for 30 percent black representation on corporate boards over a 10-year period. On the surface, 30 percent of all directorships looks like an unrealistically large number, especially when less than 2 percent of all current directorships are held by black directors.

Let us assume for the sake of argument that the top 100 companies listed on the JSE have an average or 10 directors each for a total of 1,000 directorships. Thus a 30 percent black representation would mean that over the next 10 years, blacks would hold approximately 330 directorships or a total 33 new director-ships per year. This means that only one in three companies would need to add a black director on its board in a given year. Or, to put it differently, these top 100 companies would need to add one new black director or fill one existing directorship with a black director only once every three years. I ask you, why is it unreasonable, and why should it not be done?

Representation of blacks in the managerial ranks: Our plan for increasing the proportion of black managers to that 60 percent of all managers over 10 years could not be more simple and straightforward. And yet, it encompasses all the principles of equity of treatment, equality of opportunity, and flexibility in adapting to individual company needs.

- As a starting point, we would ask that corporations promise to achieve, within the shortest period of time, a level of black hiring at the entry level of management which is equal to their representation in the overall population. Thus if the proportion of blacks in the total population is 75 percent, we would expect that, other things being equal, 75 percent of entry level managers and supervisors would also be black.

- In a number of cases, this may not be easily achieved because supervisory positions may call for certain technical skills. However, we would expect corporations to initiate on-the-job and other types of training programs to meet these targets as soon as possible.

- Once a base line has been established, all future upward promotions on the corporate ladder should reflect similar levels of promotability, i.e., if on the average, 50 percent of first grade supervisors make it to the next grade, then the same should be true of black supervisors. Furthermore, if on the average, it takes three years for a first grade supervisor to make it to the second grade, then it should also be true for black supervisors.

Information about companies' targets as to black managers, and their plans to achieve those targets, should be regularly reported in their annual reports along with other financial data and sales forecasts.

Ownership of productive assets: Nafcoc's action plan calls for the control by blacks of at least 40 percent of the total capitalization of the JSE-listed companies over a 10-year period. At present the JSE has a total capitalization of approximately $190 billion. This market is also highly liquid with less than 5 percent of the listed shares being traded in 1992. A great many shares are held in cross-holdings by companies thus creating concentration of ownership in control. It is estimated that over 65 percent of all JSE-listed stocks are represented by holdings in six industrial companies.

It is not our intention to seek transfer of wealth through expropriation or excessive taxes. Instead, we suggest that black ownership should expand through:

(a) an unbundling of current large conglomerates into economically more efficient and rational components, thereby creating greater opportunities for black ownership and control of small and medium sized companies.

(b) developing pools of capital through employee pension investment funds, sale of state-owned companies, and other public and private sources that would facilitate black buyouts of parts of these unbundled companies.

(c) creating pools of venture capital that would facilitate consolidation of otherwise fragmented, individually owned black enterprises into larger entities that may generate scale economies and also take advantage of professional management, marketing and financial services.

(d) establishing new sections within the JSE for listing emerging low-capitalized companies with less onerous listing and reporting requirements.

As an illustration, let me outline a process by which corporate unbundling might take place simultaneously with black ownership of newly unbundled companies.

1. As a first step, we would identify those companies that depend to a large extent for their sales and employees on the black community. Examples of such companies would be OK Bazaars, Score Discount Food Store, Checkers, etc.

2. These corporations would be asked to create new independent companies by putting together, for example, groups of 20 to 50 stores or one or more of their operating divisions.

3. Eventually, the same logic could be applied in other areas of business activity as well.

4. The money to buy these newly-created companies would come from ESOPs, employee pension funds, and loans collateralized by the assets of the new companies, and where desirable, by the parent company.

5. To ensure continuity of operations, the parent company would also retain a minority share in the new company's equity, and would provide it with supply contracts, and maintain other business relationships.

A similar approach can be used with foreign multinationals currently in South Africa and also with those who may be thinking of disinvesting. Companies like Shell and British Petroleum should be able to spin off groups of 100-300 service stations into independent companies. Pharmaceutical and cosmetics companies can spin off divisions comprising groups of over-the-counter drugs, cosmetics and toiletries. Other companies that are good potential targets for this approach would include Pick 'n Pay, Woolworth, hotel chains and department stores. These companies would still be linked with the parent company through purchase and franchise agreements and thus would not hurt their market position. They could actually enhance it through increased productivity, owner initiative and worker commitment.

Black entrepreneurship: The second aspect of increasing black entrepreneurship is to encourage large companies to acquire a major portion of their outside purchases through black-owned enterprises. Nafcoc's goal in this area is to reach a 60 percent target in a 10-year period. This would require a major proactive affirmative action on the part of the formal business sector not only in terms of increased purchases, but even more important, to help black entrepreneurs establish enterprises that would produce the needed goods and services.

One aspect of this program could be achieved through the unbundling process discussed earlier. However, another important part could be modeled after The Community Reinvestment Act (1977) of the United States. Under this Act, financial institutions are required to help meet the credit needs of their local communities, including low and moderate income communities, consistent with the safe and sound operation of their institutions. Community needs are broadly defined to include: quality and variety of customer services, home mortgage loans, small business loans, flexible credit, and new business start-up loans, to name a few. When a bank wishes to open a branch in a particular community, it must submit a plan as to how this establishment would benefit the affected community. Various community organizations and citizen groups are then invited to comment on the adequacy of the plan. It is only after a consensus is reached, and the Federal Reserve Bank is satisfied, that the applicant bank is granted a license to open the branch. Furthermore, banks are required to file periodic reports showing how they are meeting their commitments, and are held accountable for meeting those goals.

In the case of South Africa, companies may be required to provide, through public disclosure, details of their total outside purchases, proportions currently going to black-owned businesses, the company's targets for increasing these purchases, and the steps it plans to take in reaching those targets. We believe that a strong disclosure program would exert considerable competitive pressure and community demand to spur the companies into greater action and performance.

In closing, let me state that I realize that some of the ideas presented here would raise the level of discomfort among corporate executives. I also recognize that some of these ideas would need further development and modification before they can be implemented. However, to the extent that they provoke you into new thinking, discussion and action, they would have served their purpose.

Black economic empowerment is not merely wishful thinking. It will be a fact of life, and must be so, for all businesses that operate in South Africa. The formal corporate sector in South Africa—both domestic and foreign—has a golden opportunity to utilize its immense resources in helping alleviate the misery and economic plight of South African blacks—and we come with the plea that it do so. In return for such help, Nafcoc and the black business community will offer a willing determination to become productive partners in fruitful enterprises. We have shown that on ethical, social and economic grounds, black people are asking only what is their due and what white people already have, that is, an equal chance to prove that they are ready for, and capable of, similar accomplishments. How can we do less and still call ourselves a moral people and a civilized society?

U.S. STATE AND LOCAL POLICIES
ON SOUTH AFRICA

WILLIAM F. MOSES

You've all heard Nelson Mandela say that he'd like foreign investors to come into South Africa, but we thought we'd bring the sanctions question back to your own back yard and talk about how U.S. state and local sanctions will affect you.

In mid-September, when we prepared the 1993 edition of *A Guide to American State and Local Laws on South Africa*, we counted 179 state and local sanctions against South Africa. That was 109 cities, 39 counties and regional authorities, 30 states and the Virgin Islands.

The impact of state and local laws

Now, the first thing to remember about state and local sanctions against South Africa is that they don't actually prohibit companies within their jurisdictions from doing business in South Africa. Rather, the state, city or county won't buy products from a company that does business in South Africa, or won't invest in stock or use the banking services of a company.

The policies come in six basic varieties: Bank restriction, divestment, partial divestment, selective contracting, "Shell-free" zones, and South African goods bans.

- *Bank restriction* policies require the entity not to do business with banks that have outstanding loans or correspondent banking relationships with South Africa.

- *Divestment* requires the divestiture of stockholdings in companies with South Africa ties.

- *Partial divestment* allows divestment exemptions for companies that are signatories, say, to the "Statement of Principles" which used to be called "the Sullivan Principles."

- *Selective contracting* laws say that the city, state or county can't do business with a company that is doing business in South Africa, so they can't use those services or those products.

- As for *"Shell-free" zones*, about 11 cities and a county say that they will not use the services or products of Royal Dutch Shell, the petroleum company.

- And a *South African goods ban* is exactly what it sounds like — a city, state or county will not buy South African products.

William F. Moses is a senior analyst with IRRC's South Africa Review Service.

In our research we have found that state and local selective contracting sanctions have presented a significant barrier to businesses that have done business in South Africa or are thinking of doing business there.

For companies affected by these laws, the calculus is pretty straightforward. Essentially what you're being asked to do is to decide whether to do business with a local market — say, the City of Los Angeles or the City of Cincinnati — or to do business in South Africa. Several U.S. companies have specifically cited these laws as reasons why they cut their ties to South Africa.

But I need to underscore that these laws only affect companies that sell products to governments. If a company makes road-building equipment or sewage treatment equipment, it will be affected by such laws. On the other hand, if a company makes running shoes, gum or eyeglasses, these laws probably won't affect it much, if at all, because these aren't the kind of products that city governments usually buy.

While selective contracting is the most often cited policy that affects businesses in South Africa, many companies and many money managers believe that divestment has also had an effect, and a few companies say that when they have altered their business relationships with South Africa, they've seen their share prices go up or down accordingly. Buttressing that argument, of the 28 companies that have gone into South Africa from mid-1991 through September 1993, 15 were privately held, which of course would preclude them from being affected by divestment laws.

The process of repeal

Since Nelson Mandela unequivocally called for the lifting of sanctions on Sept. 24, a number of cities, states and counties have begun to move, and our high tide count of 179 has already come down a bit.

Los Angeles repealed its selective contracting law about two weeks ago and Austin, Texas, took a similar step about four or five days ago, although I don't think the mayor has signed it yet. The State of Wisconsin Board of Investment became the first pension fund we know of to end its South Africa restriction. Its sanction, which it repealed on Oct. 8, [1993,] said it would not invest directly in South African equities. The City of Tucson has repealed its divestment policy, too.

Action by both Los Angeles and Austin should please people who are eager to see these sanctions removed. Los Angeles in particular was one of the most serious sanctions enforcers, and a lot of cities and states have looked to Los Angeles for guidance.

In addition, New Jersey, Hartford, Connecticut, Washington, D.C., and at least 25 other localities have announced or been cited as looking into changing their policies, and I imagine the actual number is probably at least twice that big. Most notably, the New York City Council is going to consider repealing one of its laws tomorrow, and the mayor should sign it within about two weeks. The New York City Employees Retirement System is going to be considering its divestment policy on Oct. 15 and will presumably act to repeal it also.

Now, at the federal level there has been some talk of preempting state and local sanctions — it came up at House Africa Subcommittee hearings and also at a House markup on the bill on South Africa this past week — but it doesn't look very likely that this will occur. Legislators in favor of preemption say it is a way to get the sanctions mess over with, now that South Africa is moving toward democracy, so that we won't be lagging behind the rest of the world. Many in Congress who oppose the preemption of these state and local laws, though, say they believe that these laws will be repealed fairly quickly and that preemption is not really necessary. I think they're also looking at what they believe is the unpopularity and possible unconstitutionality of federal preemption of local sanctions.

The State Department, for its part, has picked a point person to help assist in the repeal of state and local sanctions and is contacting cities and states, to let them know about Mandela's statement. The ANC also says it plans similar action through the anti-apartheid movement in the United States, while the South African ambassador to the United States, Harry Schwartz, said that he has a plan to repeal sanctions and that all he needs to do is "push a button" and it will occur.

Stumbling blocks

The early evidence suggests that people are interested in removing sanctions. Nelson Mandela's position is pretty clear on this. There isn't any big movement that is opposed to getting rid of these sanctions. But there are some stumbling blocks, nevertheless.

The first stumbling block are legislative calendars. Many state legislatures are now adjourned until next spring. This should not affect the repeal of selective contracting laws, since most of these laws are not at the state level, but at the city level. But it does mean that state divestment laws will probably not be tackled until the spring and, of course, as most Americans know, even if the wheels of government are all turning in the same direction, they don't always turn that quickly.

I should add, though, that one pension board, a fairly prominent one, called us on Friday and said they're going to have a special meeting in the next two weeks to repeal their sanctions. They asked to be anonymous, but I think this is fairly typical. People are not dragging their feet on this issue.

The second major stumbling block is uncoordinated policies, and New York City and Los Angeles are pretty prime examples.

In New York City you have a city selective contracting policy that is going to be considered tomorrow, but the City Health and Hospitals Corporation and the Board of Education have their own selective contracting policies too. In addition, a number of city pension funds have their own divestment policies including the Metropolitan Transportation Authority and the Port Authority of New York and New Jersey. So while Mayor Dinkins clearly would like to see sanctions removed now, he doesn't necessarily have the right to insist on that change. The boards of these organizations have to meet. Again, there's no indication that they have any intention of not repealing these sanctions, but they don't all meet at the same time. In Los Angeles, the selective contracting policy has been repealed, but the divestment policy remains in place.

The third stumbling block concerns the opening up of old wounds. I don't think anybody in this room would be surprised to hear that the apartheid issue in the mid-eighties was very divisive for many Americans; it was not always a pleasant experience for the activists, for companies or for city council members. Many city officials therefore see the possible repeal of South Africa sanctions as a bit of a mine field, and so they may wait to hear from local constituency groups.

The last major stumbling block to lifting state and local sanctions deals with codes of conduct. Massachusetts Governor William Weld, who was the first local official to respond to Mandela's call to lift sanctions, said that he would lift his state's selective contracting sanctions, but he also stipulated that state agencies should try to purchase from companies that observe the guiding principles that the ANC released last November [1992]. Although the ANC has said that it favors unrestricted investment in South Africa, and although the head of the ANC's economic department, Trevor Manuel, says that he would very much like to see no codes of conduct imposed by foreigners, the ANC also has not repudiated the guiding principles, so the overall situation is not very clear. Since it's not very clear to us who analyze it, my frank feeling is it's not very clear to a lot of city and state governments, and so they're probably going to spend some time talking about this before they repeal.

Moreover, the South African Council of Churches, as John Lamola said earlier, has passed a code of conduct, and Rev. Leon Sullivan has said that he intends to apply pressure on companies to do the right thing in South Africa to make sure that there's equal pay for equal work. Sullivan has also announced a press conference for Oct. 20 here in Washington to discuss his intentions with the Statement of Principles, the code of conduct that he launched, but that is now run by a governing corporate council. The governing council will disband the program, as far as we know, when the multiracial elections scheduled for April 27, 1994, occur.

For now, U.S. law continues to require any American entity that controls a corporation or a business in South Africa with more than 25 employees to abide by the State Department's fair employment standards or the Statement of Principles program, but these regulations will be repealed once the U.S. president certifies that free and fast elections have taken place in South Africa. The idea, I think, behind this is to ensure that black workers in American companies would be protected by these employment standards until a democratic South African government is elected that could endorse similar standards of its own. The State Department also hopes that maintaining the current standards until elections will obviate the need for a new code.

For companies taking up Mandela's request to invest in South Africa, state and local sanctions still offer a number of challenges. However, before companies assume that state and local sanctions are going to inhibit their business activities in South Africa, they may wish to ponder the nature of the product lines they produce and whether they do significant business with state and local governments.

Some companies might also want to take a closer look at the kind of exemptions that state and local governments provide. For example, New York City has soft-pedaled its selective contracting law for at least the past year, according to our research, so as a consequence people are finding exemptions much easier to come by. In other jurisdictions, exemptions are provided for people if they join the Statement of Principles or if they have black partners in South Africa.

Another thing to look at is the laws themselves; these are the not the same laws all through the country. In Texas, for example, whose legislature will not meet again until 1995, the South Africa-related laws are particularly weak. One of the laws merely requires companies to disclose whether they do business in South Africa; the state doesn't take any action against companies that say yes.

Moreover, since a number of cities and states and counties are in the process of repeal, by the time your South African business venture is in place, this fact may be moot to many state and local entities you've done business with.

In short, I think you're going to see that state and local sanctions are going to go the way they came, which is through legislative action. While they certainly aren't going to disappear tomorrow, early indications do suggest that the cities, states and counties are actively moving to repeal their sanctions.

Update

[Since the Oct. 12, 1993, conference, state and local governments have responded predictably to Nelson Mandela's September call for the repeal of economic sanctions against South Africa. From a high of 179 state and local entities in September, the number of sanctions dropped to 78 by early January.

[Localities that moved most quickly to repeal sanctions tended to have administrative policies that executive authorities or pension boards could repeal with the stroke of a pen. Some large city councils, which meet on a regular basis, have also moved quickly. New York, with some of the country's most complex networks of local and regional South Africa policies, has completed repealing its sanctions.

[Most cities and counties have acted more slowly, partly because of restrictions on their legislative calendars and in some cases due to concerns by constituents that not enough progress towards democracy has occurred in South Africa. Most notably, the city of Chicago repealed its sanctions, but only after an acrimonious debate that pitted most of the city council, allied with Nelson Mandela's African National Congress, with supporters of the Pan-Africanist Congress, a more militant black South African political group that opposes lifting sanctions before democratic elections in South Africa.

[Most states, aside from those with administrative sanctions, have not altered their South Africa laws because their legislatures had already adjourned for the year when Mandela called for the lifting of sanctions. Most of these state legislatures are now actively considering the repeal of their South Africa legislation. In California, the most influential of the these remaining states, the state senate is considering a lower house bill that would repeal sanctions this spring. IRRC expects most other states will also act on sanctions during the first half of 1994.

[Codes of conduct remain a gray area. Massachusetts Gov. William Weld (R) has retained language referring to "guiding principles" for state selective contracting and investing. Rev. Leon Sullivan, the founder of the Statement of Principles program, told a Washington press conference in October that he was urging all states and local authorities to repeal their sanctions in anticipation of the installation of a democratically elected government, but he recommended continued monitoring of companies operating in South Africa in the new order. He argued, "we want to make sure that American companies that have remained in South Africa, and those returning, do not 'step back' in their efforts to help blacks and others with equal rights and affirmative action efforts when the sanctions have been lifted and pressure on the companies is off." Sullivan envisions using a series of "carrots" and "hammers" to ensure that "good" companies serve as examples for "bad" companies operating in South Africa.]

BIOGRAPHIES
OF THE
SPEAKERS

RONALD H. BROWN

Ronald H. Brown is the 30th U.S. Secretary of Commerce, and the first African-American to hold that office.

Secretary Brown's responsibilities in the administration of President Bill Clinton also include membership in the President's National Economic Council, in the Domestic Policy Council and in the Task Force on National Health Care Reform. He also chairs the Trade Promotion Coordinating Committee and co-chairs the U.S.-Russia Business Development Committee.

Before joining the Clinton cabinet, Secretary Brown was the chairman of the Democratic National Committee.

Formerly a partner in the Washington, D.C., law firm of Patton, Boggs and Blow, Secretary Brown also served as chief counsel for the Senate Judiciary Committee under the chairmanship of Sen. Edward M. Kennedy, and spent 12 years with the National Urban League as deputy executive director, general counsel and vice president for its Washington operations.

Secretary Brown graduated from Middlebury College, and received his law degree from St. John's University, attending at night while working by day as a welfare caseworker for the City of New York. He served for four years in the U.S. Army in both Germany and Korea.

Secretary Brown is a trustee for Middlebury College and the chairman of the senior advisory committee of the Institute of Politics at the John F. Kennedy School of Government, Harvard University. He also is an elected member of the Council of Foreign Relations.

DAVID ROBB CRALLE

David Robb Cralle is Manager for Africa/Investment Development with the Overseas Private Investment Corp. He is responsible for OPIC investment promotion programs throughout sub-Saharan Africa.

Until recently, he was the Senior Associate/Investment Development for Latin America and the Caribbean. Until 1990, he was a Political Risk Investment Insurance Officer for Latin America, underwriting American investment against political risk -- inconvertibility, expropriation and political violence. He has worked on a variety of transactions including debt-for-equity swaps, privatizations and international cross-border leasing. He has been with OPIC since 1985.

Mr. Cralle was first employed in international airline passenger marketing in New York and Los Angeles. Later, he held positions with The Chubb Group of Insurance Cos. and Citibank in New York, Rio de Janeiro and São Paulo, Brazil.

He holds a BA with Distinction from the University of Virginia. He also holds a Master's degree in International Management from the American Graduate School of International Management (formerly Thunderbird Graduate School).

LIONEL GREWAN

Lionel Grewan is the executive director of the National Economic Initiative, which is headquartered in Durban, South Africa. It is currently supported by 80 major companies and 70 small businesses. The NEI has three functional areas—advising companies on affirmative action, assisting major companies to link up with small business suppliers, and disseminating information on housing, particularly on new funding instruments and innovative housing structures.

Mr. Grewan has had a long association with U.S. companies. In 1976, he worked under contract for Bell Helicopter International and was based in Isfahan, Iran. The contract involved training Iranian student pilots and mechanics in flying and in the maintenance of helicopters. The Iranian revolution, in which the Shah was deposed, brought the contract to a premature end, forcing his evacuation from Iran.

Mr. Grewan returned to South Africa where he joined Citibank in 1981. His responsibilities included managerial development and affirmative action. He also traveled to Citibank locations in the United Kingdom, Greece, Hong Kong and the Philippines to train Citibank employees. In 1984, while remaining a Citibank employee, he was assigned to coordinate the Statement of (Sullivan) Principles program in South Africa where his role was to enhance the individual company performance of the 130 signatories to the program. After Citibank disinvested from South Africa, Mr. Grewan continued the work of the Sullivan program as a consultant until he took up his current responsibilities at NEI.

Mr. Grewan received a BA from the University of Natal. His continuing education has included the Executive Education Program at the University of the Witwatersrand Graduate School of Business and the Executive Development Program of the University of Pennsylvania's Wharton Business School.

ANNETTE HUTCHINS

Annette Hutchins is the former Director of the Soft Sheen International Foundation. In that role, she developed a USAID-funded program on education and training in South Africa. She also developed the mission and structure of the International Foundation for Education and Training, which operates in South Africa and elsewhere in Africa, and in Brazil, Jamaica and the United Kingdom.

Much of Ms. Hutchins's career has focused on economic development in Africa. From 1988 to 1991, she was the director of the U.S.-Zimbabwe Business Council, where she organized annual business delegations to the United States to meet with business, government and nonprofit leaders as well as trade missions from the United States to Zimbabwe. She also organized a meeting with President Mugabe and American corporate leaders sponsored by Coca-Cola and developed a guide on doing business in Zimbabwe.

In 1987, Ms. Hutchins served as the field director of the Technical and Material Assistance Program of Southern Africa, based in Harare, where she monitored, evaluated and developed community economic development programs. From 1982 to 1985, she served as director of the Women and African Development Program at the African-American Institute in New York City and Nairobi.

Her other positions have included: Chief of Staff to Coretta Scott King at the Martin Luther King Jr. Center in Atlanta, Director of the National YWCA's National Program Center for Racial Justice, and Director of Development Education for the Global Ministries of the United Methodist Church.

Ms. Hutchins received a BA degree in sociology from Spelman College. She recently began an MBA program at the University of Chicago.

AZAR JAMMINE

Azar Jammine is the Executive Director and Chief Economist of Econometrix (Pty.) Ltd., South Africa's leading private, independent economic research and consulting company, of which he is a major shareholder. He has held this position since 1985. Econometrix analyzes the state of the local and international economies and, with the assistance of a detailed macroeconomic model of the South African economy, provides forecasts for a wide variety of economic research on an ad hoc basis. Its client base consists primarily of more than 100 leading South African industrial and financial corporations. Dr. Jammine is also a director of the Fedsure Group, a leading South African financial institution, and of the IGI Unit Trust.

Dr. Jammine has published a number of articles in the *Strategic Management Journal* (in the UK) and in the *Academy of Management Journal* (in the US) and is a co-author of the book *McGregor's "Economic Alternatives,"* as well as co-author of *Trends Transforming South Africa*, both published by Juta's in 1990 and 1991. Dr. Jammine is also co-author of the book *The New Generation Economy* to be published by Juta's in late 1993.

Dr. Jammine began his career, after completing degrees in economics and statistics with distinction at the University of the Witwatersrand, as an investment analyst at a leading South African merchant bank (Senbank) and a leading South African stock broking firm (Martin & Co.). In 1976, Dr. Jammine completed an MS in Economics at the London School of Economics. He went on to complete a PhD in Economics at the London Business School, after which he was awarded a two-year Post-Doctoral Fellowship at the Centre for Business Strategy of the School. In order to pay his way while working on his PhD, Dr. Jammine used his knowledge of six languages to conduct numerous international business consultancy projects in Europe, North America and the Far East, covering a wide variety of industries.

JOHN LAMOLA

John Lamola, a private consultant who is also an ordained minister in the Baptist Church of Southern Africa heads the Task Force on Economic Matters of the South African Council of Churches. Formerly, he headed the Department of Justice and Social Ministries in the SACC, and served as personal and research assistant to the SACC's general secretary.

Rev. Lamola holds a PhD from the University of Edinburgh. His research interests then and now are political economy, post-Hegelian philosophy and the role of theology and the church in situations of social change. He is currently writing a book of critical analysis of the policies of the International Monetary Fund and the World Bank in Africa.

GEORGE FREDERICK LINDEQUE

George Frederick Lindeque is Executive Director (Human Resources) at Escom (the Electricity Supply Commission, a parastatal). He is registered as a Practitioner Generalist and is a Mentor of the SABPP. He serves on Escom's Management Board and as a Trustee of the Escom Pension and Provident Fund; the UNISA SBL Council, Potchefstroom University Graduate School of Business Advisory Council; the National Training Board; and the Universities and Technikons Advisory Council. He is a member of the Human Factors Management Study Committee and chairman of the Group of Experts of the Human

Factors Management Study Committee of Unipede (Committee International Union of Producers and Distributors of Electrical Energy), based in Paris. Dr. Lindeque completed the Spring 1990 Sloan School of the Massachusetts Institute of Technology Program for Senior Executives.

Dr. Lindeque has played a key role in re-positioning human resources management in Escom covering areas such as training, development, industrial relations and affirmative action.

As a member of the National Training Board, he is actively involved in the task force establishing a national training strategy. His interest in enhancing the technical skills base in South Africa led to the Nürnberg project in Germany whereby mastercraftsmen are trained for Escom.

Dr. Lindeque has established a widespread network and recently managed to arrange a successful cooperation agreement between Singapore Polytechnic and South Africa's Peninsula Technikon.

Dr. Lindeque received a BA (Hons.) degree and a Master's degree in sociology from the University of Pretoria. He received a PhD in sociology in 1980 from Potchefstroom University.

WILLIAM F. MOSES

William F. Moses, a senior analyst with the Investor Responsibility Research Center's South Africa Review Service, began working for IRRC in January 1990. Mr. Moses's professional expertise includes U.S. state and local sanctions against South Africa, South African political negotiations, U.S. policy towards South Africa and U.S. investment in South Africa. He is the author of *A Guide to American State and Local Laws on South Africa* (1991, 1992, 1993) and co-author (with Meg Voorhes) of *Corporate Responsibility in a Changing South Africa* (1991).

Before coming to IRRC, Mr. Moses worked for Technoserve, a non-profit development agency that specializes in small enterprise development in Latin America and Africa. Mr. Moses has also worked for the Alaska State Legislature in Juneau, Alaska, and served as a graduate intern in Cape Town, South Africa, with the U.S. Department of State. In 1984, Mr. Moses won a year-long Thomas J. Watson Fellowship to study "The Literary Reflections of South African Culture," in South Africa, Botswana, Lesotho, Swaziland, Zambia, Zimbabwe and the United Kingdom.

Mr. Moses received a Bachelor's degree in English and International Relations from Claremont McKenna College in 1983, and a Master's degree in International Relations from Yale University in 1988.

WYNAND PRETORIUS

Wynand Pretorius has been the head of the Department of Transport Economics at the Rand Afrikaans University since 1983, as well as the director of its Research Unit for Transport Economic and Physical Distribution Studies.

He has been involved in various research projects such as the National Transport Policy Study; the Ad Valorem Wharfage Study; projects for several private sector undertakings in respect of fleet management, fleet and vehicle costing systems, operations control systems, decision support systems, depot location systems and distribution network analysis; and projects for the Department of Transport.

Currently he is acting as project leader and promoter for several formal post-graduate studies covering aspects such as funding for transport infrastructure, financing of urban transport facilities, and economic effects of the closing of rail branch lines to small communities.

He is also a member of the National Transport Policy Forum, and he has played a key role in setting up capacity building programs in South Africa under the auspices of the National African Federated Transport Organization (NAFTO) and the South African National Civics Organization (SANCO).

Professor Pretorius obtained a BCom degree in transport economics in 1976 from Stellenbosch University. He obtained a doctorate from Rand Afrikaans University in 1981 on the subject of air freight distribution systems.

MAMPHELA RAMPHELE

Mamphela Ramphele is Deputy Vice Chancellor of the University of Cape Town in South Africa. She is the director of the Equal Opportunities Research Project and responsible for the implementation of the university's Equity Policies.

Dr. Ramphele qualified in medicine at the University of Natal in 1972 and later obtained diplomas in tropical and public health from the University of the Witwatersrand. She earned a PhD in social anthropology from the University of Cape Town in 1991.

A Black Consciousness leader in the 1970s, she was banished to Tzaneen in 1978 where she founded a model community health program.

Dr. Ramphele came to the University of Cape Town in 1984 as senior researcher in the Department of Anthropology and there became co-editor with Francis Wilson of *Uprooting Poverty: The South African Challenge*.

Dr. Ramphele has received numerous awards for her research on hostel dwellers and on adolescent violence including, with Professor Wilson, the 1990 Noma prize for publishing in Africa. She has delivered many named lectures, and has written and spoken extensively in Africa, Europe and the US on the economic and social problems of South Africa. Her most recent book, *A Bed Called Home* (1993), documents the lives of hostel dwellers in Cape Town.

Dr. Ramphele is a trustee of the Independent Development Trust and a director of Anglo American Corp. and Old Mutual. She holds honorary degrees from Tufts University (1990) and Hunter College (1984) and the Medal of Distinction from Barnard College (1991).

S. PRAKASH SETHI

S. Prakash Sethi is Professor of Management and Associate Director, Center for Management, at Baruch College, The City University of New York. Before joining Baruch College in September 1983, he was Professor of International Business and Business and Social Policy at the University of Texas at Dallas (1977-83), and Professor of Business Administration, University of California, Berkeley (1967-77).

Dr. Sethi has had extensive involvement with the democratic movement of South Africa in general and the black business community in particular. For the last four years, he has been serving as the first Economic Policy Adviser to the National African Federated Chamber of Commerce and Industry (NAFCOC), the largest and the oldest organization of black business and industry leaders in South Africa. In this capacity, he is involved in questions pertaining to the restructuring of the South African economy, the entry of black people into the formal economic sector of South Africa, power sharing, and economic relations between Southern Africa and a post-apartheid South Africa. He is a director of the South African Management Program (South Africa/New York); a trustee of the Management and Leadership Development Center (NADCOC), South Africa; and executive director and board member of the South African Black Business Development Foundation Inc. (New York).

He is the project administrator of The City of New York/South Africa Professional Development Program, a joint partnership of some of New York City's leading corporations and the City University of New York whereby fast track black managers from South Africa are brought to New York for six months of intensive on-the-job professional training supplemented by in-depth advanced management training of black corporate directors in South Africa.

Dr. Sethi holds an MBA and a PhD in business from Columbia University, New York, and an MA in economics from Delhi School of Economics, Delhi University, India.

JOHN L. SIMS

John L. Sims, head of the South Africa Free Election Fund and an independent business consultant, recently retired from the Digital Equipment Corp., where he managed Digital's recent entry into South Africa.

As vice president of strategic resources at Digital, he reported to the President-CEO and was a member of the senior operating committee of the corporation. Mr. Sims joined Digital in 1974 as Corporate Manager of Equal Employment Opportunity and Affirmative Action. He became Director of Manufacturing Personnel in 1975, Corporate Staff Manager in 1981 and Vice President of Personnel in 1984. He became a member of the executive committee in 1986 and Vice President of Strategic Resources in 1987.

Before joining Digital, Mr. Sims held a succession of management positions at Champion International Corp. and E.I. du Pont de Nemours Co. Inc.

Mr. Sims received a BS degree in Chemistry from Delaware State College and did graduate work in organic chemistry at Ohio State University. He attended management training courses at Columbia University.

Mr. Sims serves on the board of directors of the Boston Bank of Commerce, the Museum of World Art, and Freedom House, where he also is chairman. He is a member of the Governing Board of the Boston Chamber of Commerce and is on the Board of Overseers for the Regional Laboratory. He serves on the SBI Roundtable at Florida A&M and the board of governors of the American Society of Training and Development. He holds memberships on the National NAACP, the Oversight Committee of Project REACH, MassPEP, New England Tech Association, Central Massachusetts Association, The Boston Private Industry Council, Northeast Human Resource Association, and the Executive Leadership Council. He is a trustee of the National Urban League and Meharry Medical College.

ISRAEL B. SKOSANA

Israel B. Skosana is the executive director and the second-in-charge to the chief executive of the National Sorghum Breweries Ltd., the largest black-owned and -controlled company in the history of South Africa.

Before joining NSB, he served for two years as the deputy managing director of the Get Ahead Foundation, a nonprofit organization dedicated to the development of black-owned business.

From 1984 to 1988, he worked at Anglo American Corp., where he advanced to the senior position of divisional internal auditor. From 1979 to 1984, he worked at Deloitte and Touche, advancing to the position of senior accountant. Previously, he worked for IBM, in New York and South Africa.

Mr. Skosana is a director of several companies, including NSB, Servgro International Ltd., Independent Development Trust Finance Corp. and the Financial Services Regulatory Board. He is a trustee of the Chartered Accountants Endowment Trust, the NSB Education Trust, the Community Banking Project, the Get Ahead Corp., the Literacy Trust and the Goodhope Corp. Inc., and a council member of the Peninsula Technikon.

Mr. Skosana earned a Bachelor of Commerce degree in 1976 from South Africa's University of the North. His studies were funded in part by the Anglo American Group Vocation Scholarship, awarded to him on the basis of his performance on the national matriculation exam in 1973, when he finished fourth among all black South African students that year. In addition, he holds an Honors, Bachelor of Accounting Science degree from the University of South Africa, and is qualified as a chartered accountant.

ROBERT S.K. TUCKER

Robert S.K. Tucker is a director of the law firm of Edward Nathan & Friedland Inc. and chairman of the Community Banking Project. He also serves on several boards and trusts in South Africa.

Recently, he was the chairman of the Old Mutual/Nedcor Scenario Planning Team, an exercise that brought together business executives, parliamentary and extraparliamentary politicians, economists and others to consider the ways in which South Africa's political and economic transition will unfold. This led to his joint authorship, with Professor Bruce Scott, of *South Africa: Prospects for Successful Transition*, published in 1992. He also has led a team to examine, and written a plan for, a national youth service initiative in South Africa.

From 1983 to 1991, he was the managing director of the S.A. Perm, and from 1973 to 1983, he was a partner in the law firm of E.F.K. Tucker. While affiliated with the Perm, he also served as president of the Association of Building Societies of South Africa (1987-88 and 1988-89) and of the Association of Mortgage Lenders of South Africa (1989).

He received BCom and LLB degrees from the University of the Witwatersrand and qualified as an attorney in 1972.

MEG VOORHES

Meg Voorhes is Director of the South Africa Review Service of the Investor Responsibility Research Center. In her career at IRRC, Ms. Voorhes has made several extensive research trips to South Africa beginning in 1980 and is the author of numerous publications relating to South Africa. She has testified by invitation three times before committees of the U.S. Congress to assist their deliberations. Since 1990, she has also administered a consortium of U.S. universities and colleges engaged in research on South Africa.

Ms. Voorhes has also conducted research in Northern Ireland. She is co-author of a 1989 IRRC study entitled *Religion and Fair Employment in Northern Ireland: Case Studies of Six American Companies.*

Before joining IRRC, Ms. Voorhes was the executive assistant of the American Committee on U.S.-Soviet Relations.

Ms. Voorhes received her BA from Wesleyan University and has a MIPP (Master of International Public Policy) degree from the Nitze School of Advanced International Studies, John Hopkins University.

8

PLACE IN RETURN BOX to remove this checkout from your record.
TO AVOID FINES return on or before date due.

DATE DUE	DATE DUE	DATE DUE
25		

MSU Is An Affirmative Action/Equal Opportunity Institution

c:\circ\datedue.pm3-p.1